Praise For

THE UNDERGROUND GUIDE TO JOB INTERVIEWING

"The Underground Guide to Job Interviewing is a wonderful tool and resource to make preparing for your next interview a success...Todd serves as your headhunter guidance counselor, ready to walk you through the trickiest areas of the hiring process step by step. Red flags, useful websites, and very useful rules of thumb round out this book that covers everything from how to research prospective employers to how to ask insightful questions that add to your candidacy and how to negotiate your offer without giving away your hand too early on. Prepare to be entertained, enlightened, and armed for a successful job search that will help you stand out as a rarity among your peers."

> **—Paul Falcone, Author, *96 Great Interview Questions to Ask Before You Hire* (AMACOM, 2009)**

"Todd Moster was able to assist me in landing the job of a lifetime. Although, as a long-time HR Professional and Law Firm Administrator, I thought I "knew-it-all," Todd was able to help me consider interviewing techniques from another perspective...Todd's interview preparation methods not only ensured that I made the best case possible of my qualifications for the position, but helped me evaluate whether the employer and job were suitable for me..."

> **—HR Director Trained with Moster Interview Method**

"Don't read this book unless you're ready to quit your boring job and start interviewing for the one you really want. Todd Moster's mix of practical advice and good-natured silliness delivers the keys to your new corner office."

> **—David Ackert, President, The Ackert Advisory; Founder, Practice Boomers; Author**

"Don't let Todd's witty commentaries and delightful stories distract you. The Moster method works and helped land me a job in one of the toughest market in years. Using his method, I was able to genuinely connect with my interviewers and made a lasting impression."

—Environmental Attorney Trained with Moster Interview Method

"*The Underground Guide to Job Interviewing* is a comprehensive, well written, funny book that is a quick read, and will reinforce what you already know and provide you with some new tips on successful interviewing."

—Susan Wise Miller, M.A., Founder of California Career Services, award-winning National Certified Career Counselor (NCCC), a Master Career Counselor (NCDA), Certified Vocational Evaluator (CVE) and expert witness on vocational issues.

"Love it! Todd Moster has created an easy, fun, slightly snarky read on a critical topic: Job Interviewing. I can't tell you how many times I have interviewed people who really could have used this book. If you're even slightly leaning towards buying this, do it! It is packed with helpful information and is presented in a non-pretentious, enjoyable, straight-forward fashion. I wish I had something like it for my end of the desk - the employer doing the interview!"

—Faith Pincus, CEO, Pincus Professional Education CLE Seminars; CEO, Finz Advance Tapes case summaries; Author, upcoming ABA book, *Be Heard: Public Speaking for Attorneys*

"…[A]n irreverent yet essential guide for the professional looking to leapfrog the job-hunting competition…It's easier to find a job when you have a job, but it's easier still when you follow Todd's unique advice."

—Marty Rudoy, Esq., Attorney and Partner at Rudoy Fleck, Los Angeles, California

"Todd is purely a master at his craft. Having not had to prepare for a job interview for several years, Todd was quickly able to reteach me the ways of the interview world so that I landed the very first job for which I was interviewed. Todd worked with me by thoroughly covering not only some difficult and uncomfortable interview scenarios, but also by accentuating the very basics, which he emphasizes should never be overlooked. In addition to helping me portray my best self, Todd also provided some keen insight in helping make a professional assessment as to whether the employer would be a good fit for me. In the end, he was right on all fronts."

—Tax Attorney Trained with Moster Interview Method

"Todd Moster has created a gem of a book. There are so many myths out there about the interview process. Too many "experts" give advice that is akin to getting dating tips from your grandparents. *The Underground Guide to Job Interviewing* is the perfect antidote; it's timely, modern, cuts to the heart of the matter, and is written for professionals by someone who has spent years in the interview trenches."

—Gideon Grunfeld, J.D., Former big-firm lawyer and Fortune 500 HR Executive; President, Successful Career Strategies, Inc.; Founder, Law Firm University

"This timely guide is an accessible, insightful, winning presentation of hugely valuable information. Moster shows job seekers in every field how to turn interviewing—an often an intimidating, mysterious process—into a golden opportunity to shine."

—Doug Levinson, Business Consultant; Adjunct Professor, University of Southern California; Principal, Strategy that Rocks; Author, *75/25, 3/4 of an MBA, 1/4 of the Grief*

"Before my interview for a coveted position that I thought I was perfect for, I was lucky enough to be able to learn Todd's interview techniques directly from him. It was crazy, Todd predicted the majority of the questions, or slight variations of them, that I was asked. His method kept me focused like a laser on responding to my interviewers' questions one after another with substantive information about myself. He helped me understand how to give my interviewers the exact information they needed to give me the job even if the questions they asked came out of left field. Todd taught me how to stand out by not sounding like the robotic, canned-response candidates that were interviewing for the job I ended up with."

—Health Care Attorney Trained with Moster Interview Method

"Todd Moster's book on interviewing is a must-read for anyone who anticipates a job interview with any degree of trepidation. His clarity of thought guides the reader through the most important elements of the interview process. His style incorporates humor into a plethora of useful strategies and tactics. It is evident that Moster thoroughly knows his topic, and explains it in a gentle and non-threatening manner. If you are going to be going through job interviews, especially for a professional position, read this book. Then read it again."

—Bill Saleebey, Ph.D., Author, *Connecting: Beyond the Name Tag*

"Whether you're starting a business or advancing on enemy territory in a war, certain fundamentals apply. You have to know your terrain—both the roads to take and the minefields to avoid. You need a clear objective. You must prepare. And you need to work. Hard. *The Underground Guide to Job Interviewing* applies these principles to the business microcosm of the employment interview in a practical and entertaining manner. Taut, streetwise and filled with real-world examples, The Underground Guide provides a formula sure to increase the Interviewing IQ of all but the most clueless (or illiterate) job seekers."

—Charles F. Goetz, Professor of Entrepreneurship and Distinguished Lecturer, Goizueta Business School, Emory University; Serial Entrepreneur; Author, *The Great Entrepreneurial Divide, The Winning Tactics of Successful Entrepreneurs and Why Everyone Else Fails!*

"Todd worked with me to help me hone my interviewing technique and skills. Having served as a paralegal at large international law firms for many years, I had already been through many interviews before I met Todd. By asking the right questions that made me focus on my skill sets, however, Todd was able to give me a fresh perspective on the value I bring to prospective employers. His emphasis on preparation, moreover, including a review of both the questions I should ask and questions I should anticipate during a job interview, helped me to be at ease during the interview process. Thanks to Todd's interview preparation methods, I was polished and professional in every interview and am happily employed at one of the top law firms in the world."

—Senior Paralegal Trained with Moster Interview Method

"Job interviews are serious endeavors, but that doesn't mean a book about them has to be boring. Fortunately, Todd doesn't seem to feel that way either. Blending just the right amount of practical tips, theory and humor, he's put together the perfect book for busy professionals who need a crash course in job interview techniques, but don't have the time or patience for a ponderous tome. *The Underground Guide*...comes down unabashedly on the side of the job seeker, and isn't afraid to show a little attitude in the process."

—Mark Goulston, M.D., Author, *Just Listen: Discover the Secret to Getting Through to Absolutely Anyone* (AMA-COM, 2009) and *Get Out of Your Own Way* (with coauthor Phillip Goldberg) (Perigee Trade, 1996)

"Much like a television show that reveals the secrets of how magic tricks are performed, *The Underground Guide to Job Interviewing* peels back the veil of mystery surrounding the job interview. The book presents a wealth of information forged from years of Todd Moster's experience as a top recruiter in a highly competitive market as well as his own unique experience in interviews. Unlike other books written on the topic of interview strategy, Todd's Guide finds a refreshing balance between being a highly informative manual and a humorous page-turner."

—Bradley McGavin, Esq., Director of Risk Management and Staff Counsel, St. John Knits, Irvine, California

"Todd covers all the bases involved in conducting an effective interview, from the genuine importance of knowing "what do you want to be when you grow up?" to knowing your own resume so that you can respond quickly and confidently to the interviewer, and having good questions prepared for the interviewer to facilitate an effective dialogue...Along the way, Todd employs graphics which are not only hilarious but set forth important principles. Whether you are looking for a job, or looking for an employee (though Todd is clear that this is not a book for employers), you would be well-served by reading *The Underground Guide to Job Interviewing*."

—Ed Poll, J.D., M.B.A., CMC, author of *Secrets of the Business of Law*, 2nd ed., (2012) and many more

THE UNDERGROUND
GUIDE TO
JOB INTERVIEWING

THE UNDERGROUND

GUIDE TO

JOB INTERVIEWING

A Quick and Irreverent Primer for the Busy Job Seeker

REVISED AND EXPANDED SECOND EDITION: *Includes Bonus* **Preparation and Practice Guide** *with Sample Interview Questions.*

Todd Moster, Esq.

ISBN: 1478335319
ISBN-13: 9781478335313
Library of Congress Control Number: 2010916786

TABLE OF CONTENTS

- Common Sense Is Key
- This Guide Is Directed to the "Professional"
- This Guide Is Geared to Job Interviews, Not Resumes
- Sometimes, There's More Than One Correct Way to Do a Job Interview
- The Real World Is Not Always a Pretty Place
- This Guide Is for Job Seekers, Not Employers
- It All Comes Down to the Basics
- I'm Here for You

Your Internal Preparation
- What Do You Want to Be When You Grow Up?
- What Are Your Job Search Objectives?

INTRODUCTION TO THE SECOND EDITION

A great deal has happened since the First Edition of *The Underground Guide to Job Interviewing* was released in 2011. For one thing, as the economies of countries world-wide continue to become more interdependent, people everywhere now face similar challenges of recession, un-employment and a fiercely competitive job market.

Even as some countries return to growth mode, moreover, the pace of job creation is so anemic that economists are warning of a "jobless recovery" far different from past re-cession periods. So the stakes facing today's job seekers, as they face off against an increasing number of competi-tors for a smaller number of openings, are enormous. When they land that increasingly elusive interview opportunity, they'd better perform effectively. They may not get an-other chance for a long time to come.

But good economy or bad, people will continue to interview for jobs—or know family members, friends and acquain-tances in the job market. It accordingly shouldn't have been surprising that *The Underground Guide* generated a lot of interest. What *was* unexpected, however, was how the *Guide* resonated with readers of diverse backgrounds, occupations and nationalities, many of whom reached out to provide useful feedback.

People involved in occupations not specifically covered by the First Edition, for example, such as entrepreneurs and sales professionals, remarked on how readily the principles in *The Underground Guide* apply to their situations. Their input prompted the addition of material to Chapter XI which explains how the techniques in this book can be adapted to interviews for sales positions, meetings to land new clients or business, pitching a book or screenplay, and even making media appearances.

Reader suggestions also resulted in new sections on nonverbal communication, considerations on providing work references and the importance of maintaining control over one's Internet presence. The Revised and Expanded Second Edition also includes a bonus "Interview Preparation and Practice Guide." This new section, added as an appendix, provides a list of commonly-asked interview questions, along with suggestions for how to utilize those questions as a training tool during the interview preparation process.

The Underground Guide additionally proved to have an international appeal that I had not expected. Although based on my experience as an interview coach and executive recruiter in the United States, the *Guide* struck a chord with readers in other countries where, it appears, the expectations and customs surrounding job interviews are very similar. The input received from overseas resulted in the more global perspective that colors this Second Edition. It also spurred the inclusion of new material helpful to U.S. and non-U.S. readers alike, such as how to prepare for interviews for admission to a college or university, or for interviews for visa applications with consulates in the United States and other countries.

Even while adding additional material to the book, I did not appreciably increase its length. That's by design. The book is designed to be not only an informative read, but an entertaining and quick one as well. I welcome you to enjoy this Revised and Expanded Second Edition of *The Underground Guide to Job Interviewing*, and wish you every success in your job search efforts!

Todd Moster, August 14, 2012

FOREWORD
BY MARK GOULSTON, M.D.

I don't want to brag, but I know something about stressful situations. In nearly three decades as a psychiatrist and business consultant, I've trained FBI agents on how to negotiate with hostage takers; I've worked with CEOs of dysfunctional organizations; and I've helped long-warring married couples see themselves as they did when they first met. Even worse, I've raised several teenagers into adulthood.

But there's one uniquely stressful situation that nearly all of us must deal with at some time or another: the job interview. That's why when Todd Moster, a law-firm partner turned headhunter, asked me to review his book on interview tips for professionals, I read it with interest. I've known Todd for a couple of years and watched him interact with all types of people, and there's one thing I've noticed that he does well. He listens. And that's key.

If you think about it, every successful human encounter, be it a business meeting or a date, involves effective communication. And communication means more than just unloading what you want to say. As I point out in my recent book, *Just Listen: Discover the Secret to Getting Through to Absolutely Anyone,* you can't have a genuine interaction with someone unless you truly reach that person, and you'll only reach that person if you truly listen and understand your counterpart—to the point where he actually feels "felt." Do that, and you've created a connection that can work wonders.

So when Todd prepares you for your job interview, he makes it clear that it's not just about you. It's about researching your prospective employers and positions and having an accurate picture about what they seek. It's about knowing, ahead of time, what employers say and do during job interviews and why they say and do those things. It's about understanding your own strengths and objectives. Ultimately, it's about being prepared so that when you walk into the interview, you can be fully *present*, really listen, and make a genuine connection with your interviewer.

Job interviews are serious endeavors, but that doesn't mean a book about them has to be boring. Fortunately, Todd doesn't seem to feel that way either. Blending just the right amount of practical tips, theory, and humor, he's put together the perfect book for busy professionals who need a crash course in job interview techniques but don't have the time or patience for a ponderous tome.

The *Underground Guide*, instead, goes underneath the surface, fleshing out a quick lay of the land without pretense or embellishment. The product of someone who's prepared hundreds of people for interviews over the years, it comes down unabashedly on the side of the job seeker and isn't afraid to show a little attitude in the process.

So strap in, hold on, and enjoy *The Underground Guide to Job Interviewing*.

INTRODUCTION
MISTAKES ARE GOOD

PERSONNEL DEPT.

© Miken Baldwin/ Cornered

www.cartoonstock.com

"I'll keep your application on file in case something else comes up."

It was my third year of law school at UCLA. It had been a tough semester—tough courses accompanied by that plunge in attention span when you get near, but haven't quite earned, your degree. Now it was that time in the school term that made my stomach churn.

It was time to interview.

It wasn't like I was a stranger to interviews. I fancied myself a future public servant when I was in law school. I wasn't going to join one of the huge law firms that would throw a lot of money at me. I was going to join an organization that gave free legal advice to the disadvantaged, or maybe become a prosecutor or a public defender.

I wasn't going to sell out, period. That wouldn't happen until a few years later.

So, I interviewed with a city attorney's office where they threw some hypothetical situations at me similar to the ones I was used to getting in class. (Like, "If you saw someone taking two newspapers out of a newspaper machine instead of one, would you file a case for theft against the person?") It was a cake walk.

I interviewed with two attorneys from the legal department of an Indian reservation. They wore turquoise jewelry and sandals. One of the attorneys breast-fed her baby during the interview. It was an interesting experience.

Still, there was a recession on. Some agencies had hiring freezes, and there was a lot of competition for the open positions. As the year went on, I got a little worried. I needed backup. I decided to interview with some law firms after all.

And that led me to Milt Mincer. That's not his name. I haven't changed his name for privacy reasons. I just can't remember it.

Still, I remember quite a bit. The scion of a well-regarded California law firm (or so I was told), Milt kept me waiting in the reception area. I was nervous, of course, like any inexperienced interviewee waiting for his number to come up.

It didn't help that I'd walked three long blocks from the bus stop in ninety degree weather to get to Milt's office. I didn't own a car during law school and had only one suit, a heavy tweed number that had to be worn with a vest.

So I was soaking wet as I sat waiting for Milt, concerned that I smelled like a farm animal.

The reception area was decorated with drawings of old English judges wearing powdered wigs and of English aristocrats on horseback shooting foxes to death.

What a happy place.

I was summoned into Milt's office.

Milt sat behind a massive wooden desk in a huge office. Actually, "sat," doesn't quite do Milt justice. Milt had an uncanny resemblance to Jabba the Hutt of *Star Wars* fame, except not as good looking. So rather than sit, he seemed to rise like a blob of jelly above some primordial spongelike glop.

Milt had huge jowls which vibrated even when he was still. As I walked to the straight-backed chair facing his desk, his eyes followed me like a hungry lizard eyeing a fly.

Standing a little behind Milt, on either side of his jowls, were two junior attorneys. Wearing impeccable suits and neat, circa 1965 haircuts, they almost looked like brothers. Their job, as it later turned out, was to nod thoughtfully as Milt spewed out his words of wisdom.

Finally, the Great Man spoke. He said a kind word or two about my law school and introduced his two sidekicks. Then, almost in mid-sentence, Milt stopped. He swiveled his head to look directly at me.

"What kind of money are you looking for?"

Now, I was prepared for this question. My law school had an outplacement office, and one of the nice ladies who worked in it gave me a sense of the salaries being paid to first-year attorneys like me. She recommended I say something on the higher side of the range so there would be room to negotiate.

I threw out my number and stopped for dramatic effect. Milt just looked at me for what seemed like a long time. I could swear I saw the seasons change. I attempted a smile, wondering if I looked like a proud man facing a firing squad.

A stream of red flowed up Milt's jowls. "*What* did you say?" he asked, in a tone I used to hear a lot from my first-grade teacher. The sidekicks seemed stunned. They stopped nodding and gazed at me, as still as department store mannequins.

Milt softened. "Do you have any idea how *ridiculous* that number is?" He spoke in a barely contained shriek, and I wondered if he'd had any success with that voice in court.

The interview continued for twenty more torturous minutes, with Milt reciting some of his earth-shaking accomplishments and my asking a few perfunctory questions before I engineered my exit.

Which brings me to the point at hand.

You simply don't—I mean *don't*—answer the how much money you want to make question immediately, no matter how straightforward a person you are and how insistent the person asking the question is.

But more on that later in chapter 5. Back to the subject at hand. Milt.

I don't hold grudges. I hope that Milt has a long and happy life and that his keepers keep his cage fresh and clean.

The point is that there are a lot of Milts out there. Even worse, there are Milts that don't look like Milts. There are Milts that don't know they're Milts.

Your job is to smoke out the hidden Milt. He may be right across the desk from you. Maybe several Milts, both male and female, will take you out to lunch and cast wayward glances at you as they joke around and scan the room for slow flies.

Maybe, of course, you'll be lucky enough to interview at a completely Milt-free environment. Still, you always want to prepare for an interview with the assumption that you'll be meeting Milt.

That's what this book is about.

CHAPTER I
PROVISOS, EXCUSES, AND ADMONITIONS

Well, hello! Very nice to meet you, and thanks for coming. Take a seat!

It sounds like you've lined yourself up for a great interview. How long has it been since you last interviewed for a job? That long? Wow. Well you're likely a little cold in your interviewing technique, although my job is to get you warmed up and ready to go.

Truth be told, however, even if you've been interviewing nonstop over the last month, it's always a good idea to hone your interview skills. If you think about it, a job interview is one of the most important business meetings you're ever going to attend. So congratulations on turning a new page in your life and coming in to see me!

• Common Sense Is Key

I'm not going to have many magic bullets for you. What we're going to be talking about are things you probably already know, even if you haven't realized it. The key to a good interview, really, comes down to good old-fashioned common sense and knowing how to recognize a curve ball even as the pitcher begins his windup.

• This Guide Is Directed to the "Professional"

What I'm going to be telling you is the result of my own experiences and mistakes, combined with the feedback I've received from all the candidates I've coached over the years. I'm a legal recruiter and have worked exclusively with people in the legal field, such as attorneys, paralegals, and high-level administrative people. I'd accordingly expect my advice to be most relevant to individuals in the so called "professions," such as attorneys, accountants, HR advisors, architects, doctors, and others who have had to undergo extra years of formal education and licensing requirements to serve in their line of work.

Jobs that are not officially labeled as "professional," be it artist, building contractor, or automobile mechanic, are of equal or greater value to society. Since my career roots are in the professional world as an attorney-turned-recruiter, however, that is all I'm qualified to talk about. Some of my advice, in fact, would probably *not* be appropriate for people in other areas of work, such as sales people, who are often expected to take a harder, try-to-close-the-deal-now approach to job interviews.

• This Guide Is Geared to Job Interviews, Not Resumes

This guide starts with the assumption that you've already put together a solid resume, or at least one decent enough for you to line up some job interviews. Writing a good resume is an indispensable part of the job search process and a major subject unto itself. Since the purpose here, however, is to give you a quick and dirty, yet hopefully comprehensive, primer on how to interview for a job, we'll have to leave the resume thing aside for now and suggest you consult other sources.

With that said, many of the principles applicable to a good interview are equally applicable to resumes. Both are about effective and persuasive communication, after all. So I expect you'll find much of the information here to be helpful in preparing or honing your resume.

• Sometimes, There's More Than One Correct Way to Do a Job Interview

As you plow through this book with what I hope will be gleeful abandon, you may notice that my advice may differ from what you've heard from other recruiters, job coaches, or authors. That doesn't mean those other individuals are wrong. Sometimes there are several right ways to do something. All I can do is give you the tips that have worked for me and the candidates I've sent to interviews over the years, along with an explanation here and there as to why those techniques work so well.

• The Real World Is Not Always a Pretty Place

You may find some of the things I say to be counterintuitive or downright disagreeable. That's fine. This is a guerilla guide. My job here is to tell you the facts as I see them, not to earn the Goody Two Shoes Award.

A job interview is not a game, but it's also not like having a heart-to-heart talk with your grandma. It's a serious business meeting governed by mutual expectations and the sometimes illogical rules of social convention.

• This Guide Is for Job Seekers, Not Employers

If you're an employer about to start the hiring process, this book is not for you. This guide is a private conversation between a seasoned recruiter and his candidates and may include some elements that you, as a prospective interviewer, will find distasteful or even offensive. So show some decency and put this book back on the shelf, will ya?

Hmmm. You're still here, aren't you? OK, look. You're not going to find any great secrets here, just a candid discussion of the way things really are, as opposed to how we think they should be. If you remember anything after reading this guide, and I hope you don't, it's that you need to see things from the perspective of your job applicant, and treat her with courtesy and respect.

Remember also that you were once an interviewee yourself and should sympathize with those who are in the same position. In fact, you may find yourself back in the role of job seeker sooner than you think…Who's that angry man storming into your office?

• It All Comes Down to the Basics

No matter who you are, where you are, and what you happen to be doing in life, it's always a good idea to reacquaint yourself with the Basics…and I mean Basics. Some of the points I'll be covering will be so obvious, in fact, that you may feel I'm insulting you. Keep in mind, however, that I cover exactly the same steps with a job seeker, whether she's interviewing to be the General Counsel of a large corporation or a junior paralegal with a law firm. Both types of jobs are important and noble. Both involve human beings. Both involve the same principles.

• I'm Here for You

Lastly, feel free to interrupt or challenge me at any time. Since I'm giving this advice in book form, I don't expect that to be much of a problem.

CHAPTER II
PREPARING FOR THE INTERVIEW: DO YOUR RESEARCH!

© Mike Baldwin / Cornered

www.CartoonStock.com

"I see you brought a stick. I'm impressed.
You've done your homework."

Talk to any really good house painter, and he'll tell you
that a perfect painting job has very little to do with the

actual painting part. It's all about the prep. That's the way it is about most things in life...And that's certainly the way you want to approach a job interview.

So how do you prepare for a job interview? It comes down to the two fundamental aspects of life itself. There's you, and the universe. How's that for keeping things simple? In a job interview, there's you, and the universe of people with whom you'll be interviewing—and possibly spending a good part of the next few years of your life.

Let's start with the part of this equation that you really like. You.

YOUR INTERNAL PREPARATION

I know you've got some interviews coming up, and don't worry. We'll get to the nuts and bolts in no time. But first, let's talk about some of the important steps you've hopefully already taken which have to do with your internal, personal preparation.

• What Do You Want to Be When You Grow Up?

A job search is always a good time to stop, take a breath, and reassess. How did you get into your current profession, and is it really right for you?

The holy grail of society today is to find a job or profession that not only pays the bills but provides enjoyment and a sense of fulfillment. That's a great goal to have, and I want you to really think about it, because you're important and life is precious. So, if you haven't already done some soul-searching on this, do it now. Ready...GO!

"Dude, touring with a punk rock band was fun, but what I'd really like to do is be CEO of a Fortune 500 company."

Now wasn't that worthwhile? I'll bet you haven't really done that since high school. Hopefully, you've stepped away from yourself for a few minutes and really gotten a fresh perspective on things.

Still, we can't escape reality. All of us can't be employed in the profession or type of job we really love. If so, I'd be a full-time test subject in a massage school and wouldn't have the time (or likely the motivation) to write this book.

You'll hear that same message when you talk to people who lived through the Great Depression. They know that work sometimes comes down to plain survival. Whine to them about a lack of satisfaction in your job and they'll probably bark something out like, "Well, why do you think they call it *work*!"

So, maybe we can't all be in the ideal employment situation. Life is not always going to be the perfect jelly for your peanut butter. Still, there's nothing wrong with trying to find the best working situation for where you are in life *now*, even if some day you may be doing something different.

• What Are Your Job Search Objectives?

If you're thinking about leaving your current job for a new one, chances are there's something in your present job situation that's missing or really bugging you. I'll bet that even if you've been laid off and are in a more urgent job search mode, there were still things about your prior job that weren't ideal and that you'd like to correct, if possible, in your next job. Believe it or not, a lot of people don't give the potential downsides of a job change the attention they deserve. After all, a job move means that you're going to be taking on new family members. Really. And you're going to be spending as much time with the new family as you do with the "real" people in your life.

Really think, then, and I mean *think*, about what's bugging you about your current work situation, what you're looking for, and whether the new job situation you're seeking may really solve the problem.

Keep in mind that one of the first things an employer will look for in your resume is whether you've had a stable employment history. It's no sin to change jobs, of course. Almost all of us have done it.

Still, the amount of time and productivity that will be lost by an employer who trains and assimilates a new employee, only to lose her when she quits or just doesn't work out—and then starts the process anew with a new hire—can cost an employer several times the annual salary of the position involved. So if your resume shows you've been in five different jobs over the last six years, the employer's going to think you're a flight risk, however good the reasons for your job changes.

That means you need to give the core issue of whether you even have to change jobs the attention it deserves. You don't want to have yet another job change on your resume that you have to explain.

So if you haven't already explicitly done so yet, ask yourself what your employment goals and underlying motivations are. If the answer is that you don't have a clue, then maybe you ought to think twice about going to that job interview. In fact, it might be a good time to return this book. Did you keep the receipt?

YOUR EXTERNAL PREPARATION

This is the place at which most people start their preparation for a job interview, but it shouldn't be. You really need to do some self-reflection, your own life assessment, first. So if you've just skipped the prior section on internal preparation, go back and read it now. Otherwise, I simply won't go any further. That's right. This class is over.

I mean it.

What? You've already paid for this interview program? Well, it's a free country I guess (unless you happen to be reading this in North Korea), and you can do, or not do, what you want. All I can really do is give you the best advice I can, and reluctantly keep the exorbitant fee you've paid for this book.

• Do Your Research

I know that with this point, I've once again demonstrated my talent for stating the obvious. That doesn't mean that it's not a key, important, significant, necessary, serious, critical, and essential part of your interview preparation, however. Doing the right research is such a vital step, in fact, that at the risk of being repetitive, redundant, and saying the same thing over and over and over again, I'm going to give you this advice: Do your research.

Have I made that clear enough? Research, research, research the job responsibilities and the employer.

Do your research.

Research the Job Description

Where do you start? Well if you just read the subheading to this section, you know you first need to review the job description. This may mean going to the original ad or posting you saw, or, if you're working with a recruiter, having her tell you as much information about the position as possible. If you still don't have enough detail, try going to the "career" page on the employer's website, if it has one, and seeing if the job is listed there.

Of course, even with your best efforts, and lacking your having an inside source at the company, there may be only so much information available. Job applicants and their recruiters, after all, are on a need-to-know basis when it comes to employers, and the latter may simply not provide the necessary details by choice, laziness, or ineptitude.

 RED FLAG:

The lack of an adequate job description may be a red flag. It may indicate that the firm or company involved is not a good place at which to work. The essence of a productive working relationship, after all, is clear and effective communication, and if your new employer lacks that core ability, then you may be one unhappy puppy.

Speaking of unhappy puppies (or Hush Puppies, in this instance), here's an example of how poor communication can pollute the workplace. I worked at a shoe store one summer during law school. I'll have to admit that I was not the Einstein of shoe salesmen. For one thing, I often had trouble finding the shoes I needed in the back storeroom.

This situation, unfortunately, was not helped by my manager, who was not the model of effective communication. "It's in the YELLOW BOX!" she barked at me once, when I had asked for guidance as to where to find a certain loafer. Grateful for the help, however begrudgingly offered, I ran to the spot in the warehouse to which she had directed me. Stacked

there before me was shelf after shelf of yellow boxes, of every type of shoe you could imagine.

The shoe business, it turns out, was not a good fit for me. A firm or company which can't even get its act together to put together an adequate job description may not be a fit for you.

Red flags aside, if despite your best efforts you end up with only the sketchiest information about an open position, sit down with the job description you do have and write down every duty or qualification on a separate line. Then, for each point you've written down, try to extrapolate at least three or four additional responsibilities that would logically be associated with that detail, and write them down as well. You may not be able to connect all the dots, but I'll wager you'll come out with a much more complete job description.

With the more detailed job description now in hand, think of every skill, experience, or accomplishment you've had that matches each job responsibility or requirement you've laid out. Are you really qualified for this position, or would the interview, and therefore the job, be a real stretch for you? If you conclude that the shoe fits, then you can go on to the next step in your preparation.

Research the Firm or Company

You may already know a little bit about the employer, perhaps from what you read in the classified ad or posting or from what your recruiter has told you. That's not enough. You need to dig up as much information as you can.

How do you do this? Well there are whole tomes on this subject, and I bet they're as boring as hell, but basically it comes down to old-fashioned detective work.

First, do a general, Google-style web search on the firm or company. You may be surprised at what you find. Second, if the employer has a website, study it carefully, being sure to cover even those aspects of its operations that don't pertain to your job description. Consider calling the company to see if it has any promotional literature.

If you're dealing with a fairly large private or a public company, there are sources available on the web, such as Hoover's, Yahoo Finance, Google Finance, and other paid and free services. They'll provide you a compact summary of the company's business, recent market successes or failures, and executive management. If the company is publicly held, you'll be able to get a copy of its annual report on the web or by calling its investor's relations department.

There are also websites that are specifically dedicated to providing information about particular employers and which occasionally include employee opinions and scuttlebutt. Examples of such websites are *Vault.com, Careerleak.com, Glassdoor.com,* and *Wetfeet.com.*

 **COMMENT:**

Keep in mind that I'm mentioning some well-known websites to you as a possible source of information and for leads to other websites not enumerated here. I'm not associated with any of these websites and can't vouch for their effectiveness or accura-

cy. In fact, it's possible that some of them, as is the case with the Internet in general, may direct you to sources or sites that could contain incorrect or false information. The principle of "buyer beware" (or Caveat Emptor, as we like to say in the legal biz) definitely applies!

Lastly, there's nothing like good old-fashioned networking, so it never hurts to ask around to see if anyone you know—or anyone *they* know—has ever worked for the employer and can give you some inside information. Although this avenue of research is frequently not available, it's certainly worth a try. If it works, you've mined yourself some gold!

Why Research Is So Important

We've been talking about the importance of doing your research, and I've provided some suggestions as to how to go about it. We haven't really addressed *why* it's so important. Well, like a lot of things in life (and notice I'm not including relationships here), the answer is pretty simple.

There are two primary reasons for researching the employer with which you're going to interview. The most obvious reason is the one you've already thought of. You always want to walk into a business meeting—and a job interview is nothing more than a type of business meeting—knowing as much as you can about the person on the other side of the table. Otherwise, you might as well be trying to cross a minefield on a pogo stick.

The second and more overlooked reason for doing your research is that it's going to generate questions in your mind about the job and employer, some of which you'll want to ask during the interview.

It's a cliché—but absolutely true—that a job interview is a two-way street. The employer is not only evaluating whether you'd be a fit for the organization; you're simultaneously evaluating whether the organization is a fit for you.

Back in the days when I was practicing law, I talked to a partner about a deposition I was about to take of an opposing party in a lawsuit. Depositions are pretty freewheeling things. You're asking questions to someone who is under oath to help you prepare your case, but since you're doing it in the very early stages of the case, before you get to trial, you've got a lot of leeway in the things you can ask.

My partner's advice, given these circumstances, was very simple: "Be endlessly curious." That's the approach you want to take when you prepare for an interview.

To paraphrase a philosopher named Stuart Smalley, "You're good enough, smart enough, and doggone it, people like you!" You deserve to know what you'll be in for if you take a new job. The only way you can do that is by thinking about what you really need to know about the job and asking questions during the interview.

- ## Review, Rephrase, and Recite Your Resume and Experience in Detail

The Importance of Ready Access to Information

"WILL THAT BE ALL, OR WOULD YOU LIKE TO ADD A FEW MORE UMS, ERS AND AHS?"

Have you ever had the experience of having trouble recalling your own phone number, even though you know it, because you seldom call your own phone number?

Have you ever accidentally called your wife by a pet's, or perhaps an old girlfriend's, name? Have you ever had to sleep on the couch?

Chances are, if you're going to the trouble of reading this book, that you are a smart, dedicated, and hard-working individual, and you do your job exceptionally well. This means that you really know your stuff, right?

Yes and no. Sure, you know what you've accomplished in your career and how to handle your job responsibilities. That's a long way from being able to describe that experience in clear, concise, and simple terms, however.

Say you've got to explain how to drive a car to someone who's from a remote island and has never seen a car. There are likely hundreds of things you know how to do but have now become a matter of habit, such as making sure you keep your car in the lane, moving your foot from the accelerator to the brake, and keeping an eye out for the Highway Patrol when you're speeding.

The fact that you're familiar with all these things doesn't mean you'll be able to break down those details and explain them off the cuff, however. You'd be much better off if you first explicitly revisited all those important tasks you handle when you drive a car, even though you now do them automatically.

The same concept applies when you're relating your experience or qualifications to someone. Sure, you did a great job when you prepared one of your accounting clients for an audit a few years back, but what did you really *do* when you put together all the paperwork? Sure, you aced that malpractice case a few months ago, but what were the key things you said that swung the jury in your favor?

Get Yourself Ready for Showtime

How does this translate to preparing for a job interview? Take your resume out the day before your interview and read it as if for the first time. Identify each specific experience, skill, or accomplishment you've mentioned and try to recall every fact or detail that led you to include it in your resume. Do the same with any other relevant information that you might want to bring up during the interview.

In other words, go through every fact in your resume and pretend that someone who is completely unfamiliar with your profession is asking you what it means. Then articulate— whether by speaking out loud to yourself, writing down some notes, or role-playing with a friend—the actual answer you'd give to that question.

Do you really need to talk out your experience instead of just thinking in general about those things? Well, you don't *have* to do anything. But what's a politician going to do before giving an "extemporaneous" speech to a crowd? She's going to review the basics of a speech and practice how she's going to say certain things. When she then talks to her audience, she's going to sound spontaneous, organized, and persuasive.

Sound like a hassle? Well it is. But the key here is not just *having* the experience and knowledge it takes to do a job, but being able to *readily access* and *relate* that information when you're asked about it.

A new job is a life-changing event. It determines the people with whom you'll be spending half your time and the challenges and expectations you'll have to meet on a daily basis. If you're really serious about changing your employment situation, it's worth the work.

In other words, prepare, prepare, prepare. Got it?

CHAPTER III
THE DAY OF YOUR INTERVIEW: A FEW BASIC CONSIDERATIONS

I promised you at the beginning of this book that I would sometimes get so basic in my advice that you might think I was insulting you. Since I always try to live up to my promises, let's hit some of the fundamentals to keep in mind for the day of your interview.

WHAT TO WEAR TO YOUR INTERVIEW

DOCTOR FUN

It was a bad idea for Bob to wear a t-shirt to his job interview,
and it was a particularly bad idea to wear the t-shirt he wore.

Dress codes in the workplace have changed drastically since the good old days. Many offices continue to feature men and women in suits or other formal business attire. Others, both big and small, favor more casual clothing, from open shirts and khaki pants to jeans and sandals.

So what's an interviewee to do? Dress up. Wear a suit or equally appropriate attire. Do not wear culottes, and do not (you men, especially) wear a tutu.

Your decision to wear conventional business attire, of course, may make you feel a little awkward if everyone else at the company, including your interviewer, is observing a more relaxed dress code. Don't sweat it. Even if she gives you a little good-natured teasing, your interviewer will know that you've overdressed as a gesture of respect and instinctively perceive you as a careful decision maker who avoids needless risks.

In other words, it doesn't hurt to overdress.

WHEN TO ARRIVE AT THE INTERVIEW

• Don't Be Late

You never, ever want to be late to an interview. If you are, and arrive even one minute late, you will probably blow your chances. It doesn't matter whether you were delayed by an unexpected car accident or the onset of Armageddon.

I'm not saying this is fair or even makes sense. It's just the way it is. There hasn't been one occasion in which one of the candidates I sent to an interview and who was even a tiny bit late went on to get the job, regardless of qualifications and reason for delay.

Of course all of us get into a pickle sometimes. There may be an occasion when despite all your best efforts, unforeseen circumstances prevent you from making your appointment in time. If that happens, don't start sniveling or prostrate yourself at your interviewer's feet. There are exceptions to every rule. Explain what happened and hope for the best.

Still, do everything in your power to ensure that this situation does not happen. Plan for traffic accidents, speeding tickets, construction delays, and every other contingency so that you arrive at the interview site with plenty of time to spare.

• **Arrive 7–10 Minutes before Your Appointment**

As you may have gleaned from the above discussion, you don't want to be even a minute late to your interview. You also don't want to arrive too early, because the employer may not know what to do with you and may feel awkward.

Accordingly, plan to walk into the reception area seven to ten minutes before your appointment. If you arrive early at the employer's building, take a walk or get some coffee, and then walk into the reception area seven to ten minutes before the interview. That will show your promptness while giving the interviewers plenty of time to get ready to greet you.

You may ask how the seven-to-ten minute recommendation was derived. That's would be an excellent question, and the answer is that I haven't the slightest clue. It just one of those things that works!

WHAT TO BRING WITH YOU

Make sure you bring at least one copy of your resume with you to the interview. There is no reason to volunteer it to anyone after you arrive. Just have it handy in case one of your interviewers has misplaced it. At that point you can whip it out, thereby getting your questioner out of his jam (however small) and displaying your excellent preparation skills.

Some people like to bring a pen and writing pad to their interviews. That's fine too if it floats your boat. You just don't want to bring anything too elaborate, such as a laptop or pet ferret, for example, that will distract your interviewer from the key issue of your suitability for the job.

HAVE YOUR EMOTIONAL HOUSE IN ORDER

Let's face it. An interview can sometimes be a pleasant experience, but it's not fun. It's not like getting a massage. It can be downright nerve racking.

That's OK. It's perfectly normal to be a little nervous during an interview. Even the highly respected actor Sir Lawrence Olivier admitted that he was always a little nervous before stepping onto the stage. If your interviewer doesn't talk with candidates on a regular basis, moreover, it's equally possible that *he'll* be nervous as well.

Some interview and public speaking experts suggest playing tricks on yourself to calm yourself down. For example, they'll suggest you visualize your interviewer or audience as naked. I'm personally not a big fan of playing tricks on yourself. Besides, it would make me think of Milt (see introduction), and that's a place to which I'd rather not go.

Fundamentally, a job interview is a business meeting. You're hoping to establish a commercial relationship which may or may not happen. There's no death penalty for not excelling at a job interview. So at the risk of being baldly and boringly obvious, just do the best that you can. If you don't get the job, you'll survive.

CHAPTER IV
ASKING QUESTIONS

"Excuse me. Is this
the Society for Asking Stupid Questions?"

Have you ever served in the role of an interviewer—perhaps meeting with an individual who was seeking a job with your present employer?

Let's say you have, and you've finished asking your questions and completed the obligatory blather about the company and what a great place it is at which to work. (The subject of karma for the fibs we tell in life is beyond the scope of this book.) Now let's say you ask the candidate whether he has any questions for you, and the candidate answers, "No, I have no questions because you've been so thorough in telling me about the job and the company."

What would you think about this person? That he's not very interested in the job? Sure, that makes sense. Maybe he's not a very inquisitive individual, and therefore may not have the creativity and self-assurance to do his job well? That's a good guess as well. And maybe he's just a lump on a log with a spectacular lack of energy and enthusiasm for life.

Regardless of your conclusion, I'd bet you'd walk away with a fairly negative impression of that individual.

That's what you want to keep in mind when you walk into an interview. Not only do you need to ask questions to lay the groundwork for an intelligent decision if you later get a job offer, you've got to ask questions, period.

THE TYPES OF QUESTIONS YOU WANT TO ASK

- **Ask the Questions That Are Most Important to You**

 **RULE OF THUMB:** _____

It's Your Show.

If there's one underlying theme to this book, it's that you're an individual, and you count. You're not a cog, but if you have the cog mindset when you walk into the interview room, one of two things is likely to happen.

One possibility is that you won't be hired because you didn't distinguish yourself and are clearly a cog. The other possibility is that you *will* be hired because the employer wants a cog, thinks you're a cog, and will treat you like a cog once you're on the job. Either way, you'll be miserable.

Since interviewing and accepting a new job is a very personal thing, the only person who can come up with the most important questions is you, based upon your individual goals and concerns.

Cliché or not, interviewing is a two-way street, and you should not even consider leaving your current job without asking the questions that are most important to you during your job interview. If you've covered the preparation steps laid out in chapter 2, it should be a pretty easy process. Give yourself a gold star.

RULE OF THUMB:

Give yourself a gold star.

Whoops...That's not it.

RULE OF THUMB:

Know what your individual goals and concerns are before you walk into the interview room.

Still, there are some fairly common questions that can be adapted to any situation, so let's take a quick look at them.

• *How* You Ask Is as Important as *What* You Ask

There are certain kinds of questions that most people want to ask, and really should ask, during an interview. What's equally important, however, is *how* you ask your question.

RULE OF THUMB:

Ask substantive, open-ended questions about the job and the company.

An interview is all about getting information and establishing a good relationship with the interviewer. That's not going to happen if all you ask are yes-or-no questions.

Let's say, for example, you're an attorney interviewing for a position at a law firm, and you want to find out if the firm will help you attract your own clients. You can certainly ask, "Do you provide support for attorneys who want to go out and develop their own business?" The answer you'll inevitably get is a simple "yes" (whether or not it's actually true). What did you learn from this magnificent give and take? Not a heck of a lot.

Instead, you want to ask something like, "What kind of marketing support do you provide to attorneys who want to develop their own business?" Now you're cooking. Chances are your interviewer will provide you with specific examples of the client-development support the firm provides, thereby imparting truly valuable information. And if the firm really doesn't provide any real support, you'll have the fun of watching the interviewer squirm as she tries to come up with an acceptable response.

Examples of Questions to Ask

There are literally hundreds of appropriate questions that can be asked at interviews. Since the purpose of this book is to give you a quick and concise primer on interview skills, however, I'm going to provide some examples of questions below with the expectation that you'll get the general idea and then come up with your own:

a. How are new projects assigned to people in the department?

b. The job description states that a senior paralegal will be required to organize and help run the case. Since the role of paralegals can vary from firm to firm, can you give some examples of the kind of work that will be expected from the person you hire?

c. What is the reason for this position being open?

d. I noticed on your website that you provide forensic accounting services. Can you expand on that a little?

e. How many people work in this department, and what different roles do they play? Do the various departments work together, and if so, how?

f. Where do you see the company going over the next two years? Are there any specific goals you're seeking to accomplish?

g. What type of administrative support is provided to employees?

h. How would you describe the working atmosphere here?

i. How would you describe a typical day at the company (or, for someone in my position)?

j. Who do you consider your major competitors to be, and what distinguishes this company from them? What led you to choose this company over similar ones?

THE TYPES OF QUESTIONS YOU *SHOULD NOT* ASK

There are certain questions that you never want to ask during a job interview. Some of the most obvious boners are listed below, but you at all times want to remember the following.

 ## RULE OF THUMB:

If you can think of any downside to asking a particular question, don't ask it. In other words, if you have a doubt, leave it out.

Here are some examples:

a. How Much Money Does This Position Pay?

Yes, this is the big question every one of us wants and needs to know in connection with a new job. Yes, the employer knows this is just as important, and knows you know. Nevertheless, this is the proverbial elephant in the room that no one acknowledges.

Why?

It could be that raising the subject of money during the interview (as opposed to post-offer) stage may give the impression, rightly or wrongly, that all you care about is money, as opposed to working as part of a team, giving your soul and first-born to the company, blah blah blah.

The most practical answer to this question, however, is "because." Simply put, questions about money are just not asked in interviews. It's as scandalous as failing to hold out your pinky of your white-gloved hand when you sip tea with the queen. It's just not done, and for that reason comes across as vaguely unseemly.

I'm not saying any of this makes sense, so don't shoot the messenger. It's just the way it is. OK?

b. What Kinds of Benefits Do You Offer? Do You Provide Free Parking? How about Dental?

These are a sub-species of the how-much-will-you-pay-me question and should be avoided for the same reason.

c. How Often Do You Give Raises and How Much Are They?

This is yet another incarnation of the how-much-will-you-pay-me question. Don't ask it.

d. What Hours Do You Require?

While a perfectly good, straightforward question, asking it can give the impression that you're a clock watcher who doesn't want to work very hard.

e. Do You Pay Overtime? Are People Required to Work Overtime Often?

These are double-whammy questions because they combine the concepts of compensation *and* hours.

f. What Type of Training Do You Provide?

Some of the how-to-interview books actually *suggest* you ask this question. I, however, think it sucks. It suggests that you feel you're not qualified for the job, even though your intention may be to communicate how you're always willing to learn new skills to get even better at your job.

g. Have You Had the Opportunity to Read My Resume?

This is another one of those questions that some recruiters recommend you ask during an interview. I disagree.

No matter how your interviewer answers this question, there's at least an even chance that you've offended him. If the answer is "no," for example, then you're pointing out that he's stupid, negligent, lazy, or all three of those things. If the answer is "yes," he may think that you've assumed that he's stupid, negligent, lazy, or all three of those things.

The potential upside of having the person read your resume and letting you expand on its contents doesn't justify the risk. Just do your best to figure out whether your resume has been read or not, and then deal with the situation as best you can.

RULE OF THUMB:

Don't ask unnecessary questions that your interviewer can't answer or will feel uncomfortable answering.

RULE OF THUMB:

If you have a doubt, leave it out.

h. Where Will My Office Be?

Kind of presumptuous, don't you think? This question implies that you think you've aced the interview and have the job, even if that's not the case. It also puts emphasis on your personal comforts, which makes it similar to the compensation and benefits questions.

i.   When Would I Be Eligible for Promotion?

It's very understandable that you would want to ask this question. Most of us are interested in opportunities for advancement when we take a job.

On the other hand, you don't want to create the impression that you're not really interested in the job for which you're interviewing, and that you instead want to use it as a stepping stone for a higher position.

If you want to find out about opportunities for advancement, by all means ask the question, but couch it in much less personal terms. For example, you can generally ask whether there are opportunities for advancement, and if so, can they describe how the system works.

j. If I Want to Donate My Kidney and Other Internal Organs to My Immediate Supervisor, Will the Firm Support Me in that Effort?

Wow. Now how's *that* for the ultimate suck-up question?

PREPARING YOUR QUESTIONS PRIOR TO THE INTERVIEW

I don't know about you, but I don't have the world's greatest memory. (This is the complete opposite of my wife, by the way, who can recite every stupid or clueless thing I've ever said from the beginning of time.) So as smart and quick on my feet as I'd like to think I am, I'm not going to wing it when I go in for an interview.

The best analogy I can give you here goes to my background as a trial attorney. No matter how well I knew my case, I never went into court without notes and believing that, like Perry Mason, I'd be able to ask the witness the perfect questions in the right order.

I always wrote down my questions ahead of time, not because I planned to read them verbatim during my examination, but because the very process of writing them down focused me on the key issues and made my in-court presentation all the more effective. And besides, Perry used cue cards.

So, the day before your interview, sit down with your legal pad or computer and pound out a bunch of questions.

You're not going to bring those written questions with you into your interview room, of course, or even ask those same exact questions. By going through this exercise ahead of time, however, you'll be more focused on the job at hand and be able to cover your areas of inquiry in a more complete and diplomatic manner.

CHAPTER V
ANSWERING THE TOUGH QUESTIONS

OK. Here's where most people think the task of preparing for an interview begins. Unless you were on another planet during the first part of this book, however, you know that's balderdash.

Still, there's no denying that answering questions is where the action is during an interview. If the earlier stage of the prep process is like studying the pool table for all the right angles, this is the time when you pick up your pool cue and take your shot.

Most of the questions listed below come up often during interviews. No doubt you've had to answer one or more of them in the past. The fact that they're commonly asked, however, and are for the most part fairly legitimate questions, doesn't make it any easier to answer them. Let's take a look at some of the more challenging questions.

FREQUENTLY ASKED TOUGH QUESTIONS

- ## How Much Money Are You Looking to Make?

"I'd like to make $3.2 million a year, but I'll settle for $8 an hour"

Of all the cheesy questions that get asked during interviews, this is the Limburger of them all, so we're going to spend some time discussing it.

RULE OF THUMB:

Do everything humanly possible to avoid directly answering this question.

How am I going to do that, you ask? I'm going to give you some strategies for answering this question. In fact, I'm going to give you a *Plan A-1*, a *Backup Plan A-2*, a third *Backup Plan B*, a fourth *Backup Plan C*, a fifth *Backup Plan D* and yet a sixth *Backup Plan E*.

The Problem with the Money Question

It seems perfectly logical for an employer to ask a job seeker what she's seeking in compensation. So what is it about this question that makes it such a landmine?

The question is problematic for several reasons. For one thing, no matter how much prior research you've done before your first interview, you will probably not have an accurate fix on what the employer is willing to pay, either generally for any person in the position or for you in particular.

So being forced to throw out the first number in that situation can hurt you in two ways. It can result in your inadvertently asking for an excessive amount of compensation for the position, which will immediately remove you from consideration. It can also result in your asking for too little, which may exclude you from consideration for being unqualified or naïve or ensure that any offer the employer ultimately extends will be unreasonably low.

More fundamentally, and whether rational or not, there's just something unseemly about having to discuss money during the interview process—at least before a formal job offer has been extended and negotiations have commenced. It's kind of like the need to use deodorant in the morning. It's an important part of modern etiquette but not necessarily something we want to talk about.

When the Money Question Comes Up

There are some situations in which the money question is more likely to be asked than in others. Let's say you're interviewing with a really small firm or company, a mom-and-pop establishment, for example. Since salary represents a much larger component of their bottom line, they're going to have a better reason for asking the question. They don't want to waste their time or yours, so if you two are very far apart, they want to find that out at the earliest possible time.

This question comes up during interviews at bigger firms and companies too, although not as frequently and with less good reason. Sometimes the main interviewer will ask you directly. Some executives or partners, however, prefer someone else to do the dirty work, and will have the designated HR person ask the money question for them.

 RED FLAG:

Keep in mind that just as an interviewer may view a candidate who asks about compensation during an interview as inordinately concerned with money, the same may apply to an employer who can't wait to lay that question on you. If money is one of the first things you're asked about during your interview, it could very well be a red flag that the company views its employees as commodities and that it may not be the right place for you.

The Game Plan for Answering the Money Question

a. Plan A-1 (If You Have a Recruiter):

If you have a recruiter in your corner, then you've got a built-in advantage when you're asked the money question. That's because of the way recruiters work when they represent a candidate: We not only send your resume and "pitch" you to the employer, we coordinate all interviews and, if the employer decides to make an offer, negotiate salary and other matters on your behalf. So if the issue of compensation comes up, it's really for us to handle—although obviously in consultation with you.

OK. So you're sitting in the office of the Hiring Partner of Wei, Pei, Les & Les. She's very gracious, and you've been having a nice conversation about your mutual interest in golf. You're beginning to relax. She smiles, leans forward, and as if offering you a bon bon, gently asks you, "How much are you looking to be paid?" Then, like any smart lawyer or salesperson, she stops, leans back, and stares at you.

Your answer should sound something like this:

> *Well, as you know, I was submitted to you by Todd Moster from the Best Agency, and he instructed me that if issues such as compensation came up, to immediately refer the question to him, since that's something he prefers to discuss with his clients. So if it's OK with you, I'd like to refer this question to Todd.*

This response will usually stop your questioner in her tracks. As likely as not, she'll smile and just move on to another subject.

Why? There could be many reasons. For one, you're describing the way a diligent recruiter works, and if she respects that individual and the process, she'll back off when you remind her of the relationship.

Second, almost every interviewer has at some point been an interviewee and realizes how unfair the compensation question is. With just a little push back, you've politely pointed that fact out, prompting your questioner to make a dignified retreat.

 ## RULE OF THUMB:
Many employers haven't the slightest idea how to properly interview someone.

Think about it. There's no school that teaches people how to interview candidates, and most individuals, including many HR people, simply wing it. That's why there's so much turnover in business. With such poor interviewing skills, employers end up hiring the wrong people.

And that's not such a terrible thing, by the way. If everyone did such a perfect job in the hiring process, there would be no turnover and no need for recruiters. So God bless them, I say.

But I digress. The above method, while often effective, doesn't work every time. Your inquisitor may be determined to get an answer one way or the other (see Rule of Thumb directly above) and may ask it again, perhaps in a different way, or even circle back and zing you with it again later in the conversation.

Not everyone uses a recruiter to get a job interview, of course. In fact, most people apply for jobs directly, and therefore can't use the recruiter as a buffer for avoiding the compensation question.

So whether you don't have a recruiter, or you do but Plan A-1 didn't work, that's when you go to Plan A-2.

b. Plan A-2 (When You Don't Have a Recruiter, or When You Have a Recruiter, but Plan A-1 Didn't Work)

Plan A-2 amounts essentially to a three-part answer, each segment of which you'll adapt to your own situation, values, and style.

1. Concede that compensation is important.

    Let's face it. Unless, perhaps, you're Paris Hilton, compensation is always a big issue when you're considering a new job. You can be just as sure, however—whether it makes sense or not—that the money issue is like that unspeakably horrendous singer who makes his way into your subway car with an accordion and open hat. He's there, all right, but you don't want to acknowledge he's there.

    So you might as well as admit the obvious, but make it clear that compensation is not the be-all and end-all for you. You're not a shallow person, after all (and if you are, skip to Plan Y below), and there are other things that you value in a job. That's what takes you to the second part of your answer.

2. Describe some of the other features you're looking for in a new job.

Yes, we all need money to live. We have to support ourselves and our families. But compensation is seldom the *only* reason for taking the inconvenient and unpredictable risk of starting a new job.

So think about what you really want to gain or accomplish in a new employment setting. Do you want to take your professional development to a higher level that's not available in your current situation? Are you looking for a company with its own marketing department that's dedicated to helping its employees develop new business? Is the company a leader in an industry—say, renewable energy—that interests you?

Think also about what's less than ideal in your current situation, and then turn it into a positive attribute that you'd like to be part of your new job. If, for example, you're working at a place where everyone closes the doors to their offices, and it is as quiet as a tomb, perhaps you're looking for a work culture in which people more freely interact and exchange ideas. Maybe you're at a company that has been slow to embrace new ideas and technology, and is about to be left in the dust by its competitors (one of which may be the company you're interviewing with!).

Whatever your reasons or goals in seeking a new job, identify and crystallize them during your interview preparation stage. Then take two or three of the strongest ones and recite them briefly in this part of the answer.

3. <u>State that you're willing to consider a reasonable offer.</u>

Hopefully, you've communicated the above points in your own way, and done so effectively. Now it's time to take the conversation back to where your interviewer started it—compensation. So bring the subject up again, and make it clear it's a subject you'll seriously consider in the context of all of the other key aspects of the job.

Example: You're back in the Hiring Partner's office at Wei, Pei, Les & Les, and, as if the question just occurred to her, she innocently asks, "What kind of salary are you looking for?" It's time to put the plan into action.

> [PART 1:] *Well, needless to say, compensation is always an important issue when one is considering a new job. [PART 2:] At this particular stage in my career, however, there are other considerations that are equally, if not more, compelling. I'm looking for a firm that represents large clients in more high-stakes litigation; has a reputation for excellence; and that has the kind of nice, supportive people that I'd look forward to joining every day. [PART 3:] Based upon the research I've done on your firm, it's clear you have all those attributes. So if you decide at some point that I'd be a good member of your team, I'm sure you'd come up with a reasonable offer, and I'd be happy to consider any reasonable offer.*

 **COMMENT:**

Concerned that if you follow the above formula your answer will sound stilted or canned? You shouldn't be. Remember that unless you've done

the required soul-searching, and have a genuine handle on your wants, needs, and objectives, you have no business interviewing for a job. This three-part structure is simply a suggested way to effectively present your case. If you truly know yourself and your goals, you'll make the answer your own and do fine.

c. Plan B

You've landed that interview, either on your own or through a recruiter. You've executed Plan A-1 or A-2 perfectly and done everything you can to avoid answering the compensation question. Unfortunately, your inquisitor keeps coming at you like a politician running for a TV camera. "I appreciate that answer, John, but I also want to make sure you and I aren't going to be wasting our time if we take this process further. So what's it going to take for you to join us?"

Yikes. Here's that question again. What do you do?

Stick to your guns. Give your interviewer the same answer, in a shorter and modified form.

> *I totally understand your concern, and recognize that compensation is always a key issue. As I said earlier, however, I'm putting a higher priority at this point in my career on ___, ___, and ____. That's why I'm certain that if you decide I'll be a good fit here, you'll come up with a reasonable proposal, and I'd be happy to consider any reasonable proposal.*

 ## COMMENT:

Some people prefer to answer the money question by saying that they're looking for something "competitive." It's not a terrible answer, I suppose, but I'm not crazy about it.

The word "competitive" conveys the subliminal message that you're a striver, a grasper, a climber for the money, and that's really the only thing you care about... And everyone knows that you haven't the least interest in money, and that all you want is the opportunity to give yourself, body and soul, to your next employer, right? Well, wrong, but as we've seen before, the desire for money is that dirty universal truth that for some odd reason, as a social convention, we want to avoid articulating during an interview.

 ## ANOTHER COMMENT:

Concerned that you'll look stubborn and uncooperative by not just coughing out a number like a trained seal? Well, there's always that risk. One can never predict how another person will react in a situation. That's what makes being human so interesting and challenging.

On the other hand, you're a person of principle (aren't you?). If you instantly fold on a position you've just firmly, and hopefully eloquently, stated, what will they think of you? So my recommenda-

*tion, as the song goes, is to tell your story and stick
to it—that is, unless you have to go to Plan C...*

d. Plan C

The Greek Philosopher Socrates was famous for responding to every question, or answer to a question he had just
asked, with yet another question. His relentless style of
questioning, designed to help his students uncover universal truths, had profound implications. For one, it changed
the course of Western Civilization. For another, it inspired
a form of torture, known as the "Socratic Method," that
would plague generations of future law students. For yet
another, it drove the exasperated authorities of Ancient
Athens to devise a response that even Socrates could not
rejoin with yet another question—a bracing drink of poi-
sonous Hemlock.

If your interviewer continues to press for an answer to the
money question, a mild and polite version of the old philosopher's method may be just what you need to move
the conversation to a more productive track. Answer her
question with a question of your own such as, "Can you
tell me the salary you have in mind for the position?" or
"I assume you have a compensation range in mind for
this opening. Can you give me a ballpark range of what
you've budgeted for the position?"

The meeting-a-question-with-a-question technique is not a
guaranteed way to avoid the money question, of course.
It has, however, been known to prompt the occasional
interviewer to back-off or pursue a more fruitful line of
questioning. And in certain situations—especially when
the person with whom you're meeting is not experienced
in questioning job candidates—the interviewer may simply

blurt out the compensation range for the position, giving you a strong tactical advantage if things proceed to the job offer stage. Should the interviewer suddenly produce a goblet and offer you a drink of an ancient Greek herbal concoction, however, it would be best to decline.

e. Plan D

Yeesh. You've done everything you can to avoid the compensation question, but your interviewer just won't let up. It seems apparent, unfortunately, that you'll have to throw that pit bull a slab of meat, if only to give yourself a chance to take a breath.

Where's the beef? It's your current compensation level. Tell your tormentor what you're making, and then restate Plan B in a somewhat different and briefer fashion:

> *Well just to give you a sense, my current base compensation is $120,000, but that's, of course, at a different company which operates under a different set of facts and assumptions. But like I said before, sure, compensation is always important, but it's really not the be-all and end-all for me. I'm looking for a place where [and insert what you're looking for here, very concisely] and you seem to be that kind of place.*

f. Plan E

What if the pit bull is still hungry? What if it keeps charging at you for a tasty dollar figure? What do you do?

There are three solutions. You can (1) politely leave the interview; (2) distract your interviewer by riding a unicycle and playing a kazoo; or (3) throw out a number.

Chances are that, having read this book, you will have done your preparation and will provide as reasonable a compensation figure as you can based upon your assessment of the value of your work, your knowledge of the company's size and other individual qualities, and the research you've done on the compensation being paid to others in a similar field (on websites such as *Salary.com*, *Payscale.com*, and the salary search page of *Indeed. com*, for example). Once you've stated your number, concisely rephrase Plan B, stating that compensation isn't the only factor in your search, and quickly reprise your main job search goals.

Then jump for cover.

 **COMMENT:**

Conducting research on competitive compensation rates is a tricky business and beyond the scope of this book. Suffice it to say that with the exception of large businesses which pay fairly uniform salaries based on the individual's experience level or title, companies can be all over the map with regard to compensation.

All you can do under such circumstances is what your mother would tell you—your best. If a vein starts throbbing on your interviewer's forehead, or some building security people appear, chances are you may have overstated your case. If that doesn't happen, you're at least still in the game.

RED FLAG:

As a recruiter, I don't work with candidates whose first and only concern is compensation. There's nothing wrong with that motivation, of course, but—for reasons of personal satisfaction, if nothing else—I prefer to associate with people who respect the professional and personal qualities that allow us to grow as human beings. In other words, I'm going to work much harder on behalf of a person who's seeking a collaborative work environment and opportunities to share his/her knowledge than someone who is exclusively after a 10 percent raise.

And I feel the same way about employers. An interview *really is* a two-way street. If an interviewer were to incessantly harp on the subject of compensation during my interview with him, I'd conclude not only that the employer cares about money—which is perfectly fine in itself—but does so to the exclusion of everything else. Absent dire financial circumstances (in which case all bets are off), I'd consider the prospective employer to have flunked the interview from my point of view. I'd politely endure the rest of the process and get the heck out of Dodge at the earliest opportunity.

RULE OF THUMB:

The individuals an employer chooses to actually sit down with and interview job candidates reflect the firm's office culture. If those interview-ers display personal traits that are incompatible with yours, such as an air of condescension or an obsession with compensation, chances are the employer and the job are not for you.

• What Are You Currently Being Paid?

For all the years I've been in the recruiting business, I have yet to figure out a way to avoid answering this question. It's a perfectly reasonable, if unwelcome, question that most employers will ask at some point in the process.

So what do you do?

Some recruiters will counsel you to simply decline to answer the question, or to say that you think your employer would prefer to keep that kind of information private. There is often no single, correct way to handle an interview question, and perhaps one of these approaches will work for you.

I don't buy it, however. You've been asked a direct question about an objective fact. All you can do is give a direct and truthful answer.

There are of course downsides to giving such a straightfor-ward answer. If you're currently being paid a fairly low sal-ary, for example, there's a chance that the employer will use that number as a starting point and make an offer that undervalues your worth. If, on the other hand, you're being paid a healthy salary, you may be taking yourself out of con-sideration with an employer who could never pay that much and will assume that you'd be resentful and unproductive if you came in at a lower salary.

Certainly, if you feel it appropriate, you can qualify your answer by stating that you understand that every company/ firm is different and no two jobs are ever exactly alike. More-over, should you be aware of facts that may cause your present salary figure to be lower or higher than what your interviewer's company may be paying—say, your present company is significantly smaller or located in a lower-paying geographical area—then bring them up in your answer.

Part of my job as a recruiter, as it was when I was a lawyer, is to point out the boulders in my candidates' and clients' paths, even if they'd prefer not to look at them. The com-pensation you're receiving is as much a part of your profes-sional life as your DNA. If you can add some provisos about your current salary that makes your case stronger, great. When you get to the bottom line, however (literally, in this case), the only reasonable way to answer the current-com-pensation question, in my view, is to tell the truth and let the chips, as the cliché goes, fall where they may.

• **Why Do You Want to Leave Your Current Job?**

There are variations to this question, of course. If you're an accountant with a longtime solo practice, you'll be asked why you've decided to leave your current situation and join a firm. If you're a partner seeking a partnership elsewhere, you'll be asked a similar question. If you're an in-house attor-ney or paralegal looking to join (or rejoin) a law firm, you'll be asked why you want to leave the corporate sector for the indescribable pleasure of billing for your time.

Whatever form this question takes, there are two things to keep in mind. First, there *is a 99 percent chance that this question will be asked by someone during your interview.*

Second, I'm going to give you a three-part guide to answering this question that seems to work pretty well. Let's go.

1. <u>State that you like your current employment situation and quickly cite two or three examples that support your case.</u>

   Employers don't want trouble. They want to bring in someone who's comfortable in his skin; will train easily; assimilate easily into the office culture; and be a productive, longstanding member of the company.

   That's why employers tend to avoid applicants who have a great number of job changes on their resumes. They're concerned that the candidates will never be happy, regardless of the situation, and are therefore a flight risk.

   Similarly, if someone who's lucky enough to have a job (as opposed to someone who's been laid off or is otherwise unemployed) has only negative things to say about her current work situation, that person will be viewed as a malcontent, even if those objections are well founded.

   As miserable as your current employment situation may be, there *have* to be some positive aspects to being there. Otherwise you wouldn't have stayed there for as long as you have—or displayed abysmal judgment when you made your original decision to accept that job.

   That's why you need to say some positive things about your present job—and make sure you're sincere when you do.

The positive attributes you mention can be as varied as your work environment. Perhaps you've got a great relationship with your immediate supervisor, or have found it exciting to be at a company climbing into the Fortune 100. Maybe you enjoy the camaraderie that comes with working long hours with colleagues, even if those hours result from chronic understaffing at the firm.

Whatever you say, make sure it's genuine. The job interview equivalent of "It was a pleasure being part of a pool of such talented people...So what if it had a few sharks?" is not going to cut it.

"MAYBE YOU COULD REFER TO YOUR TIME BEHIND BARS AS 'LIVING IN A GATED COMMUNITY.'"

2. <u>Describe why, despite all of the wonderful things you mentioned in the first part of your answer, you're looking for another employment situation.</u>

This is the meat of your response to the why-are-you-leaving question. That's why it's positioned here, like the beef in a hamburger, between the two buns of the first and third parts of your answer.

Everyone knows that you wouldn't be interviewing for a new job if everything were hunky dory at your present place of employment. The key is to describe those problems in the most positive light possible.

Maybe you've benefited from the excellent training in a large company that's known for its micromanagement and are ready to step up to the plate and take on more responsibility. Perhaps business has been slow, and you're alarmed by all of the empty offices around you. Maybe the firm insists on using antiquated organizational tools, when more high-tech, efficient options exist.

Whatever you say, make sure it's truthful *and* diplomatic. Do not bewail your work environment or badmouth any current or former supervisors or colleagues. If your concern is with lack of opportunities for advancement, for example, don't state it in negative terms such as "I'll never get promoted there." You might as well be scuba diving with a Cadillac tied to your back.

Instead, couch your answer in gentler terms, such as, "The company tends to operate as it always has, with people doing the same duties in the same job, and with very little movement. So as much as I like my present job, it's always nice to have the possibility of advancement, and I don't see that in the cards any time soon for me or, really, any of the other people with whom I work."

3. Explain why the position for which you're interviewing is a good fit for you, and you for it.

This is where you tie everything together. Take some of the less-than-satisfactory aspects of your present job that you described in part 2 of your answer and explain how the job for which you're interviewing addresses or solves them.

If you're the long-time chief operating officer of a mid-sized company who has mastered every part of the job, and are interviewing for a similar job at a much larger, international company, tell them that you're ready and excited to take on a new challenge and explain how the person-to-person emphasis of a smaller workplace can be successfully employed in a larger working environment.

You can also cite some of the positive attributes of your personality and explain how they can benefit your new employer. If you're always exploring new ways to develop business, for example, and are interviewing at a company known for its innovative advertising campaigns, point out the similarity.

Needless to say, you're going to have to adapt the three-part-job-change answer to your own situation, and relate it in your own words. Let's look at three examples to help you get the hang of it.

Examples:

The Free Rider Scenario: You're a founding partner of a small accounting firm where you really enjoy and respect your colleagues. As the years have gone by, however, you've become the primary rainmaker, with your colleagues contributing little, if any, new business. You're a little tired of continuing to split the compensation pie equally when you're the one who always buys the ingredients and bakes it. Now, you're sitting in front of the Hiring Partner of a much larger firm who asks you, "Why do you want to leave your current firm?"

> [PART 1] I'm very proud of the success my firm has had over the years, and I love working with my partners, who are all great accountants, colleagues, and friends. [PART 2] As the firm has grown, however, I've evolved into the primary rainmaker, and can't seem to convince my partners to undertake serious client development efforts. I've accordingly concluded that this is the right time to take my career to the next level and go to a larger firm where my partners are respected for both their practice and business-development skills. [PART 3] Having researched your firm, I know you offer the variety of practices and infrastructure to support active client-development work, along with the congeniality I enjoy at my current firm. I'm excited by the prospect of combining my practice and clients with yours and creating the kind of synergy that I know will help grow my current business exponentially.

The Greater Responsibility Scenario: You're working as a litigation paralegal in the legal department of a Fortune 500 corporation. The company and its legal department are so large that everyone works in a defined legal area. You, for example, handle all product liability cases against the company. That's fine as far as it goes, but you'd love to expand your expertise and job variety by working on some of the interesting business and patent disputes handled in other parts of the legal department. When you volunteer to work on some of those other cases, however, you're told you're the best paralegal they've ever had in the product liability area and that everyone needs to focus on their assigned task. Now, you're interviewing with the Director of HR of a smaller company. Off-handedly, in the middle of a conversation about the weather, she asks you why you want to leave your job.

> *[PART 1] I've been thrilled to be at a company like International Whoopie Cushion and play a role in the many contributions it makes to society. The attorneys and supervising paralegals are wonderful to work with, and the software systems we use are state of the art. It's also fun to be part of such a huge and busy legal department. [PART 2] The legal department is so massive, however, that the lawyers and paralegals are compartmentalized into defined practice areas, such as product liability, intellectual property, and real estate. I love what I do, but I entered paralegal work because of the variety of challenges that the career offers. Now that I've mastered all the details in my product liability area, I've decided it's time to go to a place at which I can take on additional responsibilities*

and reach my full capabilities as a professional. [PART 3] I see that you have a legal department in which everyone pitches in and wears several hats. That's exactly the kind of challenge I'm looking for.

The Papillion Scenario: You're a fourth-year associate at a top national law firm. It's given you the opportunity to work with some of the sharpest and most successful attorneys in the country. The firm's abiding philosophy, "assume nothing; trust no one," reflects its prudent approach to client representation. Unfortunately, the motto embodies how people in the firm relate to each other and reflects a resistance to delegating authority to less-experienced attorneys. In other words, you feel like a prisoner on an isolated tropical island. You have to escape! Now, you're sitting in the office of the Managing Partner of a small boutique law firm. He asks you why you're looking for a new job.

[PART 1] I feel very fortunate to be at a top firm like Mizz, Rhee & Payne. It's given me the opportunity to be trained by some of the smartest attorneys in the business and turned me into an excellent lawyer. [PART 2] The firm has such a deliberate and hands-on approach to supervising associates, however, that it's a little reluctant to delegate authority to associates. [PART 3] I'm accordingly looking for a firm which offers the same quality of legal work, but which also encourages its lawyers to truly take ownership of their work. From what I've seen and heard today, your firm will give me the opportunity to step up to the plate and take my professional development to the next level. That's why I was very pleased when you invited me to come in and talk with you.

COMMENT:

What if you were fired from your job? That's as tough a question as it is a predicament and not readily addressed by general rules. Still, the three-part structure should be helpful. Start out by stating two or three positive features of your last job and company. Then—and here's the hard part—explain the extenuating circumstances involved in your termination as clearly and concisely as possible. If you know former supervisors who are still willing to give you a reference, be sure you volunteer that information as well. Then, in the third part of your answer, explain the valuable lessons you've learned from the situation and express appreciation for the new possibilities it's opened up for you, including the opportunity to meet with your interviewer.

- **I Notice from Your Resume That Before You Started Your Current Job, You Worked for the Fine, Dahl, Lupe & Whole Accounting Firm. Why Did You Leave That Firm?**

This question is nearly identical to the Why Do You Want to Leave Your Current Job question, except it's directed to a point further back in time. Consequently, you want to answer it with the same three-part structure, except in a briefer fashion:

[PART 1] I really enjoyed working for Fine, Dahl, Lupe & Whole. I loved the people and the firm's dedication to doing first-rate work, and I learned a tremendous amount in working for the individuals and small companies it ser-

vices. [PART 2] Having interned at a Big Five Accounting Firm while earning my degree, however, I've always been interested in working for larger clients on more complicated matters. [PART 3] My present company recruited me with a promise to give me that more complex work and kept it, so it turned out to be a great move for me.

In the event you're asked about even earlier job changes on your resume, use the same three-part structure, making your answer briefer and briefer the further back in time you go.

• **Why Do You Want to Work Here?**

This question is yet another subspecies of the Why Do You Want to Leave Your Current Job question. It can be amply addressed by the third part of the answer to that question you've already devised, although phrased a little differently or with an additional point or two thrown in.

• **Questions beyond Your Expertise**

As qualified as we'd like to think we are for a position, no one knows everything (except for my wife, who will be reading this and is an expert on all things large and small). So what do you do when you're asked a question about something that's beyond your expertise?

Don't fake it. You'll get caught, either right then or when you're ensconced in a job for which you're not completely qualified.

Instead, admit you haven't faced that exact situation, and try to come up with an example of a similar challenge or problem that you met and solved.

TRICKY QUESTIONS

These are the questions that don't sound as direct and challenging as the Tough Questions we talked about above, but can really trip you up if you're not careful.

• What Would You Say Are Your Greatest Strengths and Weaknesses?

I bet you're already rolling your eyes. Although not asked as frequently as the Why Do You Want to Leave Your Current Job question, the Strengths and Weakness question is certainly asked enough. It's usually spewed out by individuals who haven't the slightest idea what to ask during an interview or by those who should know better. Regardless of why it's asked, it's a question that, based on my informal poll of candidates, is universally detested.

This question consists of two parts, the first of which we can dispatch quickly.

Strengths:

The answer to this question should be obvious, or you have no business being in your current job, much less interviewing for another. The key to responding to this question, as with all others we're discussing, is to plan your answer ahead of time.

Perhaps you have excellent rapport with people, or excellent organizational or supervisory skills. Whatever your strengths, just don't wing it on this answer, even if you're someone who is fast on your feet. Otherwise your answer may come out as seeming shallow, incomplete, rambling, or otherwise lacking in conviction. As with every aspect of the interview experience, you need to prepare, prepare, prepare.

Weaknesses:

"I suppose my one weakness is
I'm too forthright ...Tubby."

Here's the fun part. You want to come up with weaknesses, but *only* weaknesses that are *really strengths*. In so doing, you should avoid negative words and finish on an upbeat note. The best way to illustrate this principle is with some examples.

Examples:

Problem with Delegating Responsibility

<u>Bad Answer</u>: *I guess if I had to come up with a weakness, it would be that I'm not very good with delegation. I'm always so concerned with quality that it's hard for me to let others handle important things.*

<u>Criticism</u>: I can't conceive of how someone can give this answer without sounding like a nasally, whiny, sniveling bore. Sure, you're trying to say how important it is for you to do a good job. But you're using very negative, self-destructive terms ("...I'm not very good...") to do it, and describing a quality that can be self-defeating in the workplace.

<u>Better Answer</u>: *I've been working pretty hard on my delegation skills, because work quality has always been the number one goal for me. Since productivity and efficiency are equally important, however, I've been making a point to assign out more projects and to take the time to mentor my colleagues. I've been surprised by how rewarding it's been, and the excellent work product it's produced.*

Taking Too Much Time to Do Things

<u>Bad Answer</u>: *It sometimes it takes me too long to do things because I'm a perfectionist.*

<u>Criticism</u>: Now that's a way to take strength and turn it into a weakness!

<u>Better Answer</u>: *Well, I've got to admit that I'm a bit of a perfectionist, and that sometimes I'll put in a little more time to handle things than some of my peers. I've always found it important to dot the "i's" and cross the "t's" so that things are done right the first time, however, and it's a strategy that has proved effective for me over the years.*

Lack of Organization

<u>Bad Answer</u>: *Well, I'm not the most organized person in the world when it comes to paperwork, and my desk is never going to win an award for neatness. I'm very good on my feet, however, and seem to get more done than the people in my office who have clean desks.*

<u>Criticism</u>: You're taking a trait that almost all of us have, a lack of neat-as-a-pin organizational ability, and using it to strike a common chord with your interviewer. Assuming your interviewer is not a compulsive neatnik—in which case you've already begun that long walk to the exit but don't know it yet—you've emphasized your efficiency and displayed a gentle sense of humor. Still, lack of organization, even when you try to limit it to a messy desk, is never a desirable quality, even to someone who shares that weakness. The comparison of yourself to the clean-desk cultists in your office, moreover, only makes you look petty.

<u>Better Answer</u>: *Well, my days tend to be a whirlwind of activity, and because I'm good at thinking on my feet, I get a tremendous number of things done. Still, I respect the power of advance planning and have been structuring more and more pre planned activities into my work*

 ## COMMENT:

I know, I know. You're concerned that when you respond to this question with weaknesses that are really strengths, your answer will sound canned. There's some truth to that, but the downside of seeming a little too prepared and poised pales against trying to appear "honest" and stepping into an empty elevator shaft.

Believe it or not, the unorganized desk issue came up during the 2008 presidential campaign. In a debate during the Democratic Primary, the assembled candidates were asked to describe their weaknesses. Then-Senator Barack Obama, who was the first to be asked that question, gave the honest answer that his desk is a mess, and he was always losing paper. As a result, he was criticized by one of his opponents as someone who lacked the managerial skills to be President.

As then-Senator Obama himself later put it:

> *You notice that people who've been in Washington too long, they don't talk like ordinary folks. We had this debate in Las Vegas, and somebody asked me, "What are your weaknesses?" So I said, "Well, you know, I don't keep track of paper that well, I'm always losing paper, my desk is a mess." And then they asked the next two candidates. And one candidate says, "Well, my biggest weakness is I'm just so passionate about helping poor people." And then the other one says, "I'm just so impatient to help the American people solve their problems." So then I realize well, I wish I'd gone last and then I would have known... I'm stupid that way, I thought that when they asked what your*

biggest weakness was, they asked what your biggest weakness was. And now I know that my biggest weakness is I like to help old ladies across the street.

Barack Obama
Interview with the WIP Internet News Service, March 20, 2008.

 ## COMMENT:

So what's the moral here? Honesty is of course to be preferred at all times and in all things. Without intending to be cynical, however, such bare-bones self-criticism is rarely the rule in day-to-day social discourse, except perhaps in therapy or, if you happen to be Catholic, in confession.

Think about it. Whether you're taking a position in a letter, arguing in court, explaining an error to a boss, providing candid criticism at the insistent request of a close and sensitive friend, or explaining a faux pas you committed during a date, you're going to use your social and language skills to paint mistakes or failings in a more positive light. Similarly, while an interview is certainly a place to be honest, it is not an occasion to engage in morbid self-reflection.

Moreover, the fact remains that many of our greatest weakness are also strengths. Perhaps you're a little gentler than you should be when confronting a subordinate about a serious mistake, and that sometimes causes the problem to last longer than it should. Still, you're a caring, respectful person and want to give that individual the opportunity to save face and correct his own conduct without your having to resort to harsher measures. Maybe you feel guilty about leaving work an hour early, and not getting as much done as you would have wished, because you want to spend some quality time with your daughter. You've clearly made a decision that reduces your productivity, but done so to serve a cause you see as much more important.

No doubt you, like nearly everyone in the world (except for my wife, who will be reading this sentence), have many weaknesses that may not be quite so beneficial. Nevertheless, unless your interviewer insists on a complete, comprehensive answer to this question, and sets aside the hours (or in my case, months) necessary for you to describe all your failings in detail, you have the right to use your good judgment to choose the weaknesses that are most relevant to your job and which also, incidentally, underscore your suitability for it.

OK. Time to get off my soap box and hit another tough question—and it's a real doozy.

• What Do You Like Least about Your Present Job/ Profession?

This question comes in different forms. It may also be phrased as follows:

- What's the Greatest Challenge You Have in Your Current Job/Profession?

- What Would You Improve about Your Current Job/Profession If You Could?

- What's the Worst Thing That's Ever Happened to You in Your Job/Profession?

- Tell Me about the Worst Experience You Had to Deal with in Your Job/Profession.

- What's the Biggest Mistake You've Ever Made in Your Job/Profession?

- What Really Bothers You about Your Job/Profession?

- What's the Worst Dispute You've Had with Someone in the Workplace, and How Did You Deal with It?

However this question is couched (the above list is not exhaustive) and however sincere it may appear on the surface, there are two immutable facts about it that together comprise a:

RULE OF THUMB:

1. *It is a trick question.*

2. *If you answer this question as your instincts would tell you—in a straightforward, honest fashion—you will get killed.*

Why is this a trick question? Because it presents a no-win scenario, not very much unlike the question "When did you stop beating your husband?"

An interesting aspect of this question is that the person who asks it often doesn't realize it's a trick question. Regardless of whether your guide innocently or deliberately escorts you to the edge of the cliff, however, you're going to be in one heap of trouble unless you watch your footing.

Have I gotten your attention? Let's look at a couple of examples.

Examples:

The "What Do You Like Least" Scenario:

Let's say you're a business litigation attorney having an interview with another law firm. Part of your interview includes lunch at a nearby Italian restaurant so you can get to meet some of the other attorneys. The atmosphere is comfortable, the group convivial, and you're enjoying yourself. Then, like a meatball plopping on a lap, one of your companions drops this question on you. "So what do you like least about your job?" Your answer:

> *I enjoy the practice of law and pretty much like every-thing about my firm. I guess if there were one thing I'd pick out, however, is that being a litigation attorney means, almost by definition, having to explain the law to people who are not lawyers, and since the legal system, as we know, sometimes doesn't make sense, it can take a lot of time. Still, I don't mind that much. It's just part of the job.*

What's wrong with that answer, you ask? In fact, it sounds pretty innocuous doesn't it? But let's say one of the attorneys at the table once supervised a less experienced attorney who just didn't have the patience for "civilians" (i.e., non lawyers) and as a result failed to ask a question that led to a disaster when the case went to trial. You've now been lumped in with that individual, whether fairly or not, and have marked yourself as someone who lacks the social skills to work well with clients.

The "Worst Mistake You Ever Made" Scenario:

One of your other companions at lunch jokes about how she once accidentally left her client's sensitive file in the opposing lawyer's office and almost had a heart attack high-tailing across town to retrieve it once she realized her mistake. As everyone laughs good naturedly, including an amused colleague who snorts water through his nose, she asks you what's the worst mistake you've ever made at work.

Your answer:

> *I once was working so hard and had pulled so many all-nighters on a case that I walked into a deposition one day and realized that I had prepared to question an entirely different witness! Maybe it was all the adrenaline, or because I knew the case inside and out, but I just plowed ahead and took one of my best depositions ever!*

This answer may not be great, but it's not terrible either for an off-the-cuff response. You've shown your sincerity by bringing up an event that was not trivial, but not altogether uncommon and certainly understandable. Plus, your story demonstrated your dedication, hard work, and ability to shine in the face of adversity.

Someone else at the table, however, may be an attorney with a more deliberate style who does not have your glibness and may feel resentful or jealous of your performance. Another may feel that you showed a lack of attention to detail that could lead to problems down the road. Either way, you've just learned the truth of another popular saying: There is no free lunch.

So how do you deal with this conundrum? Just keep the following in mind as you formulate your response:

RULE OF THUMB:

Answer the What Do You Like Least/Worst Mistake question with an example of an event which was: (1) totally out of your control, but which (2) you then brought or which came to a successful conclusion.

Examples:

The "What Do You Like Least" Scenario: Let's go back to our hapless litigation attorney fighting off a future case of heartburn at the Italian restaurant. To the question, "What do you like least about your profession?" he answers:

> *I love being a litigation attorney, but if I had to cite one aspect that could be improved, it would be that the court system is so cumbersome that it often takes longer than one would wish to accomplish something relatively simple. Although I regret the additional expense and inconvenience this can cause clients, we have to do the best we can with the system we've got—until we can make it better.*

See? We've got an admission of a serious problem, but it's not of our own making.

The "Worst Mistake You Ever Made" Scenario: Another example comes to mind. I once ran the "worst mistake" scenario by a corporate attorney who recounted an incident in which he was headed to a sensitive meeting that had been scheduled to close a huge transaction. He thought he left himself enough time to get to the meeting, but he found himself trapped in a massive traffic jam. He did not make it to the meeting—which was scheduled to start in the World Trade Center moments before the September 11, 2001 disaster.

Now, this story sounds so outlandish as to be apocryphal, but I have no reason to disbelieve what this candidate told me. More important for our purposes (and even though the successful conclusion here was more by accident than by plan), it succinctly demonstrates an event that's beyond our control.

• Where Do You See Yourself in Five Years?

"Where do you see yourself in five years?
Still looking for work?"

This question sometimes comes up toward the end of an interview, often when your interrogator has exhausted her questions sooner than expected and feels the need to kill time by throwing a few hokey questions your way.

You don't have to be an Einstein to answer this question, but you still need to give it some advance thought. Suppose you try to address the question with a little humor: "I intend to be rich, retired, and relaxing on a tropical island." Many prospective employers might think that answer reflects a frivolous attitude toward your work. Others, like Milt (see introduction), will have no sense of humor and have no idea what you're talking about.

The key to answering this question is to give it more respect than it deserves, and provide a sober response that reflects a serious but not slavish dedication to your profession. If interviewing for a junior accounting position, for example, you can state that you look forward to developing your expertise to the point of becoming a "go-to" resource inside the firm on tax exemption issues and a respected expert on that subject outside the firm.

• What Are Your Hobbies or Outside Interests?

This is another one of those innocuous-sounding inquiries that can put you on the train to oblivion without your even realizing you've gotten on board.

Most of us, except for Milt (see introduction), understand that people have interests outside of work and that such interests make them more interesting and resourceful colleagues. But an interview, as we've seen, is a through-the-looking-glass world with its own rules and where the laws of common sense don't always apply.

MITTELSTADT

www.CartoonStock.com

"Sometimes *I* wanna rock
and roll all night
and party every day — but
I wouldn't list it under
'career goals.'"

If you answer that question with a shopping list of active, time-consuming hobbies, for example—such as snow skiing, mountain climbing, or traveling—an interviewer might conclude that you're going to be taking a lot of vacations or don't have the give-my-soul-to-the-job attitude toward the job that he does. You may be very proud, moreover, of the work you've done with Pyromaniacs Anonymous, but this may elicit a less-than-enthusiastic response if you mention it during an interview.

My recommendation? Prepare your answer. (Surprised I said that?) You certainly need to say *something*. A person who says she doesn't have any outside interests may be viewed just like someone who doesn't ask any questions at an interview—a lifeless slug without curiosity or enthusiasm about the world around her.

So definitely be prepared to describe some of your interests, but stick with the ones, such as seeing movies, gourmet cooking, or jogging, that are more conventional, less time-consuming, and not controversial.

ILLEGAL OR INAPPROPRIATE QUESTIONS

© Mike Baldwin / Cornered

www.CartoonStock.com

"We're looking for a tough, aggressive guard dog. Have you been neutered? No, wait – I'm not allowed to ask that."

Federal and many state laws (such as the Civil Rights Act of 1964 and the Americans with Disabilities Act) prohibit interviewers from asking questions about your race, religion, gender, sexual orientation, disability, age, ethnic or national heritage, marital status, whether or not you have (or expect to have) children, religious beliefs, political views, organizations to which you belong, or the state of your health.

There are exceptions to all rules, of course, and this is no exception. If a job requires certain types of physical challenges, for instance, such as lifting boxes or climbing up ladders, you can be asked whether you have any physical conditions that would interfere with your ability to do the job. You also cannot be asked about whether you've been arrested, but you can be asked about the occurrence and nature of any criminal convictions.

So what do you do if you're asked one of these illegal or inappropriate questions? It depends on the circumstances. You always have the option of informing the interviewer that his question is improper and you won't answer it. You'll be on perfectly firm legal ground. Since we live in the real world, however, we know you've created an awkward moment (even though it's not your fault) that could exclude you as a candidate for the job.

So let's say your interview experience has been positive up to that point and that your questioner may have inadvertently stepped over the line. Consider whether you want to answer the question directly. The fact that an interviewer is prohibited from asking for certain information doesn't mean you can't volunteer it yourself.

If, for example, you remark on a nice picture that shows your interviewer with his children, he may ask whether you have any children as well. If you do and you love to talk about your kids, then feel free to say yes, and possibly create a bond with your interviewer based on a mutually shared interest.

Let's say you have young children, however, and don't want to create the impression that you'll need to leave the office frequently to take them places or attend to emergencies. You can then provide a more diplomatic response saying that you have a great family and are fortunate that it's never interfered with your ability to do the job.

 ## COMMENT:

Be aware of the hidden question. It's not unheard of for an interviewer to innocently throw out a political comment about her kids, current events, or a religious belief. Resist the temptation to respond in kind, even if you agree with her! Instead, simply keep smiling or gently change the subject.

RED FLAG:

Always keep in mind that an interview is a two-way street and that you should always trust your gut (which in my case could benefit from a few sit-ups). If you're asked more than one illegal question, or otherwise feel that your interviewer is fishing for improper information, it may indicate that your interviewer is so wrapped up in squeezing the maximum amount of work from you that he's willing to ignore the law and invade your personal life. You will be well within your rights to let the interview play out and leave, never to return, or to inform your questioner that the interview has made you feel uncomfortable and that you'd like to end it.

HOW TO RESPOND WHEN THE EMPLOYER EXTENDS A JOB OFFER DURING THE INTERVIEW

It's not unknown for an employer to make an offer to a candidate during the course of an interview. It may have even happened to you in the past.

An offer that comes during an interview is certainly a positive and complimentary development. It also presents a tricky situation.

What do you do? If you're interviewing for a dream job and the offer is reasonable, then go ahead and accept the offer. There's nothing to be gained by making a perfunctory request for time to consider the offer if it's not necessary.

There's no need to play hard to get. Far from disrespecting you, the interviewer will view your quick acceptance as confirmation of his own good judgment and as an expression of your enthusiasm for the job. In other words, you'll be off to a good start.

More than likely, however, you'll want time to think about the offer or want to wait to see if offers may be forthcoming from other companies with which you've interviewed. In that case—and assuming the offer is not so ridiculously low as to be insulting—you'll want to say something like this:

> *Thank you so much for making that offer. I've been very impressed by my experience here and am very interested. When would you like to hear back from me?*

Then, see what your interviewer says. While there's no set custom and practice regarding how much time an employer will give a candidate to consider an offer, a one-week period is eminently reasonable, and a two-week period is very common. So if you really need the time, ask for it. If the interviewer asks for an answer within a week, but you want a little more time, feel free to suggest a specific day the following week for you to get back in touch with her.

 RED FLAG:

Beware of the interviewer who expects an answer right on the spot or insists that you decide within a day or two. Perhaps he'll add that he's considering another strong candidate and needs to make a decision quickly.

It's possible that his request for a quick answer reflects a perfectly legitimate need to bring someone in as soon as possible and presents an opportunity that you don't want to miss.

"If he has a pulse, hire him!"

On the other hand, an interviewer's insistence that you provide a hasty answer may be a sign that he's desperate because something is wrong with the job. It's also an indication that he doesn't have the patience and minimal respect to allow you to make a careful, reasoned decision—an attitude that will likely carry over to the workplace.

The bottom line is that you'll have been placed in an uncomfortable situation, whether intentionally or not, and will have to make the best decision you can based upon the circumstances and your gut instincts.

OTHER UNEXPECTED QUESTIONS

"Have you ever gone to prison and if not, Burrows, Klein & Smith would like to know if you'd be willing?"

Try as we might, there is no way to anticipate every question or situation that may come up in the course of an interview.

That's OK. If you do your preparation, you'll be prepared for almost every question.

And besides, there's something to be said for not being able to predict every question in advance. A job interview is not the most fascinating thing on earth. A little spontaneity and unpredictability will keep things more interesting for you.

CHAPTER VI
ANSWERING SUBSTANTIVE QUESTIONS

Sure, every interview has its share of tough questions. That's why we often fixate on them before doing the rest of our preparation. And that's why I covered that subject in the last chapter.

Satisfied? I hope so. But we don't want to let our obsession with the tough or improper questions, however well founded, get in the way of your preparing for the substance of your interview. Questions about your *experience, qualifications, skills, and smarts to do the job*, after all—which given my talent for stating the obvious, I'm going to call **"substantive questions"**—are key to an employer's ability to evaluate your suitability for their job.

Don't be misled by the fact that substantive questions seem, and usually are, more straightforward than the tough questions. Don't assume that you know your own experience and skills so well that you can just wing your responses on the spot. If you fail to prepare your answers to the substantive questions, you're every bit as likely to be blown out of the water as if you fail to prepare yourself for the tough ones.

TYPES OF SUBSTANTIVE QUESTIONS

Substantive questions fall into two broad categories—Time Interval Questions and the Fact and Issue Questions:

1. <u>Time Interval Questions:</u> These are questions that seek information about what you've done *over a certain period of time*. They typically come in the form of:

    •   What Were Your Responsibilities When You Worked at Steele and Hyde?

    •   What Did You Do during the Six Months between Leaving the Steele Firm and Joining Son and Phun, Inc.?

2. <u>Fact and Issue Questions:</u> These are questions that probe your specific experience or knowledge in certain areas; follow up on events or skills mentioned in your resume or during your interview; or otherwise seek the who's, what's, where's, how's, and why's of your story. Some examples of these questions are:

    •   Tell Me about Your Experience Handling Class-Action Cases.

    •   How Do You Go about Preparing for an I.R. S. Audit?

    •   How Many Big Real Estate Deals Have You Negotiated on Your Own?

    •   Describe the Steps You Take When Getting a Client's Patent Issued.

- How Do You Handle Things When a Corporate Officer Wants to Take a Step That You Know Will Get the Company in Trouble?

PREPARING FOR SUBSTANTIVE QUESTIONS

I'm not sure if I mentioned this before, but you've got to prepare for every interview. You need to do this work even if you just interviewed for another job yesterday or are coming back to the same company for a second interview.

The key, as we talked about in chapter 2, is not just knowing the answer to a question. It's being able to provide that answer immediately and clearly, without having to roll your eyes up and access the information right there on the spot.

Think about it this way. An airline pilot certainly knows how her aircraft works and how to operate it. That's not going to cut it. She's going to repeatedly rehearse every possible scenario during her training, nearly every day, so that she'll be ready to take the right action without delay when the situation calls for it.

THE FIVE RULES OF THUMB FOR ANSWERING SUBSTANTIVE QUESTIONS

Poor finish to a long-winded explanation.

There are five fundamental principles to keep in mind for answering substantive questions (and for that matter, the tough questions). They're obvious, common sense rules, and the chances are you instinctively know them.

Still, you'd be amazed how many people don't follow these rules and screw up their interviews. So to keep you from joining those folks in the Land of Interview Mediocrity, let's get right to those,

 **FIVE RULES OF THUMB:**

Every answer you give to a substantive question must be:

1. **R**esponsive to the question asked;

2. **C**omplete in and of itself;

3. **I**nteresting;

4. **U**pbeat; and

5. **C**oncise.

I'm going to talk about each of these Rules below, but first, to help you remember them, let's come up with an acronym to help you keep the Five Rules in mind:

1. **R**emember,

2. **C**ats

3. **I**tch

4. **U**nless you

5. **C**lean them.

Hmmm. I've never been good at acronyms. Shall we try again?

1. **R**ummaging through

2. **C**andy

3. **I**s

4. **U**seful for

5. **C**orpulence.

OK. I know that's not wonderful either. Let's give it one more try, or feel free to whip up one of your own:

1. **R**idiculous acronyms

2. **C**an

3. **I**nstill

4. **U**nbelievable

5. **C**ontempt.

As you've doubtless already concluded, I'll never be asked to write *The Dummy's Guide to Acronyms*. Be that as it may, let's get to the heart of these important...

 **FIVE RULES OF THUMB:**

Every answer to an interview question must be:

1. Responsive to the question asked

The key to being an effective, accomplished professional—or human being for that matter—is the ability to really listen to what another person is saying. Being a good listener communicates many positive attributes about your personality, notably focus, intelligence, and respect for the individual with whom you're conversing.

Simple, right? Totally obvious, right? Then think about the many people to whom you've directed a question, only to receive a completely off-base, rambling, and useless answer. I interview hundreds of smart, experienced professionals every year and get unresponsive answers by the truckload.

So what's the solution? It's totally simple. *Listen* to the question and answer *only* that question. Do not allow yourself to veer off the subject. Do not ramble. Do not tell war stories. Do not try to be funny. Do not use a simple question as an excuse to launch a thousand examples of why you're such a swell person and perfect for the job.

Any questions?

2. Complete in and of itself

What do you expect when you ask someone a question? Well why the Sam Hill did the chicken cross the road? To get to the other side, right?

So what do you want when you ask a question? You want a *complete and satisfying answer* that's going to get you across the road before the farmer realizes you've flown the coop.

If the question calls for a brief or yes-or-no answer, such as whether you've ever used a particular word processing program, then say yes or no—and stop.

If the question calls for a more elaborate response, such describing how you handled a certain situation, then describe what you did, giving your answer, if possible, a beginning, middle, and end.

3. Interesting

Most interviews, like most jobs, are not thrill-a-minute affairs. Still, if you're being asked something beyond a yes-or-no question, make your answer as unique, relevant, and engaging as possible.

4. Upbeat

This is another obvious, although crucial, rule. No one wants to bring a negative, dour, or pessimistic person into their work family. Provide the information being requested in as positive a light as possible.

5. Concise

This is the Mother of All Rules to keep in mind when you're answering an interview question. We live in an era of extensive time demands and short attention spans. Your qualification for the job, under such circumstances, will be judged on your ability to communicate relevant information in a clear and succinct manner.

Given the importance of this issue, in fact, I'm going to give you a **Rule of Thumb** for this **Rule of Thumb.**

RULE OF THUMB:

Try to answer every question, no matter how broad, within forty to sixty seconds.

There are exceptions to every rule, of course, and you—as the person in the trenches during an interview—will have to make the call about how extensive you want your response to be. Still, your goal should be to complete every answer within the forty-to-sixty-second time limit.

Let's start with an example of one of the broadest questions possible. I've worked several years, and placed several attorneys, with a General Counsel of a large national company. He invariably starts every interview with the following question: "Tell me about yourself."

Are you cringing yet? If you've ever been hit with this question—and many of us have—then I'm sure you are.

How the heck do you provide a concise answer? Technically, the interviewer is asking for your whole life story. Chances are, however, he's not going to be very interested in hearing about your earliest memories of being pulled in a red wagon or your pride at being elected captain of your bowling team.

The way to tackle this question, then, will be to provide a professional/work-based answer that has a beginning, middle, and end. Let's say you're a human resources administrator at a small company applying for a more responsible position at a large corporation:

*I've always been fascinated with how people inter-
act with one another, especially when they're in
groups. That's why, after I received my undergradu-
ate degree in psychology, I went on to earn my master's in human resources. Fortunately, it didn't take me
long to get my first HR job at Departures International,
and I found I took to the job right away. Having now
had the opportunity to handle nearly every HR issue
out there, including hirings, terminations, workplace
supervision, and benefits coordination at a small company, I'm ready to apply all I've learned in a larger,
more challenging corporate environment. That's why
I was very pleased when you asked me to come in to
meet with you today, and I am very excited about the
opportunity.*

Let's say you've been in your current job for seven
years, say as a litigation attorney at Whynes, Nivel &
Wale, and have applied to be the Director of Litigation
for a large company. During your interview with the General Counsel of the company, she asks you to describe the
responsibilities you've handled at your present job.

On the surface, this sounds like a much narrower question
than the "tell me about yourself" question. When you think
about it, however, you've handled thousands of different
challenges during your seven years at your firm and could
probably teach a year-long college course just on what you
did when you were there.

But providing a detailed, step-by-step account of your career
history here, complete with footnotes and parentheticals,
is just not going to cut it. Instead, provide an answer which
summarizes your duties and accomplishments in broad gen-
eralities, and then leave it to your interviewer to ask follow-up
questions:

I've worked on a variety of cases at Whynes Nivel, including employment, real estate, business, and patent cases. It's been a great experience working with some of the best legal minds in the country and having the opportunity to handle every aspect of my cases, from filing the case through depositions, law and motion, settlement talks, and trial.

Having provided an expansive, comprehensive description of your time at the firm, your interviewer can now ask more specific, follow-up questions, such as the type of real estate cases you've handled. Since such questions will be intrinsically narrower, they'll be easier to answer in a briefer fashion, and you'll be off to the races.

 ## COMMENT:

Keep in mind that while conducting an interview may not be as distasteful to an employer as getting one's teeth pulled without anesthesia, it's no picnic either. Most employers view interviews as a necessary evil that can be tedious and take time away from more productive work. If you provide brief answers to broad questions, it will give your interviewer plenty of opportunities to follow up, making the interview experience a much more interactive, engaging, and pleasant experience.

 ## ANOTHER COMMENT:

The Five Rules of Thumb are of course perfectly suited to answering Time Interval Questions. Fact and Issue Questions, while narrower, may still cover

a lot of ground and therefore need to be answered, at least initially, in a hit-the-highlights manner.

 ## YET ANOTHER COMMENT:

Have we talked about the importance of preparation? If you've put in the time to anticipate the substantive questions that may be asked in an interview, and explored ways to answer the questions in a forty-to-sixty-second time frame, you should be ready to hit almost any broad question they throw at you right out of the park.

CHAPTER VII

THE OTHER 50 PERCENT OF A JOB
INTERVIEW: FIT

"We have an opening that will suit you
pefectly. It's marked Exit."

We've spent most of our time up to now talking about the kinds of questions to ask, and the kinds of answers to give, during job interviews. That's a damn important subject and is no doubt the reason you picked up this book for a quick read.

Believe it or not, however, the verbal part of an interview—the questions, answers, and factual information exchanged—covers only 50 to 60 percent of what an interview is about. The other 40 to 50 percent has to do with a more subliminal but equally important issue—*Fit*.

What's Fit? Well certainly not me. I need to do more exercise. But chances are the minute you saw the word, you knew exactly what I was talking about in the job-interview context.

Fit is the umbrella term for whether your personality, work style, and general outlook on life are compatible with that of the employer. From the perspective of your interviewer, it comes down to an even more basic inquiry: Do I really like this person? Would I feel comfortable spending eight hours every day with him? Would I enjoy going out to lunch with him or sharing a cup of coffee or a stronger beverage after work?

And Fit, like anything else in a job interview, is a two-way street. Are the job responsibilities, company culture, and compensation structure suitable for you? Do you think you'll really feel comfortable with your new work family?

Needless to say, if you've been out of work for too long and need to get a job—any job—then Fit will probably play a minimal role in your decision-making process. If there's any choice at all involved in your decision, however, Fit should and will play a vital role in your consideration of an opportunity. At the risk of repeating myself (something I tend to do more and more as I get older), and at the risk of repeating myself, a job interview is a two-way street, and your objectives and preferences are every bit as important as those of the employer.

When you arrive for your first interview, of course, you're not going to have much of an idea of whether the firm or company is a Fit for you. How do you increase your chances of making a good impression on the interviewer while assessing whether her firm is a Fit for you? There are a few steps you can take, and lucky for you, I'm going to spell them out below.

• Do What Your Mother Would Tell You to Do

We all know, or are supposed to know, the fundamental rules of protocol when you first meet a potential employer. Stand up straight. Give your interviewer a firm handshake. Look her in the eye.

Am I ringing any bells here? I sure hope so. And for God's sake, make sure you wash your face!

• The Interview Begins the Moment You Walk into the Reception Area

The moment you walk into the reception area of an employer, the interview has begun. The receptionist is every bit as much a part of an organization as the Managing Partner or CEO, although perhaps with slightly different responsibilities. In fact, he may play a more active role in your visit than you think.

Back in the days when I was a partner at a law firm, I would of course interview new prospective attorneys, legal secretaries, and paralegals. After the interview, I would always go out to the receptionist and ask her what she thought of the candidate.

The feedback I received was occasionally hair raising. Perhaps the individual talked rudely to someone on his cell phone as he was waiting. Perhaps he thought he'd make productive use of his down time by whipping out his dental floss. Regardless of the specifics, the observations she shared, if worrisome, could be as decisive for me as the individual's resume and interview.

I now apply the experience I gained as an interviewer every time I visit a client in my role as a recruiter. For one thing, I do my flossing at home. More importantly, I'll make a point, as soon as I arrive, to engage the receptionist in a little light banter. The content of the conversation doesn't really matter as long as it's brief (say a minute or so—you don't want to monopolize his time) and innocuous—the weather perhaps, or the view from windows in the reception area, or the artwork on the walls. The point really is to break the ice and make myself, and the receptionist, a little more comfortable with our new social relationship.

There's another important reason to chat with the receptionist, and it also happens to be a

RULE OF THUMB:

The person whom a firm or company chooses to be the first point of contact with the outside world will almost always be a reflection of its corporate culture.

Everyone, of course, can have a bad day or be a little grumpy sometimes (except for my wife, who will be reading this and is never, ever, grumpy). If the receptionist with whom you're interacting seems truly nasty or snooty, however, he may very well be personifying the company's corporate culture. If so, you should be grateful because you've learned early on that the place is not for you.

The take-away (as they love to say in the sales biz)? Keep your eyes open. In fact, let's take that a step further.

• Be Observant

As you're being escorted to an office or conference room for your interview, make a point to absorb as much of the atmosphere as possible. Are people smiling or walking around with sour expressions on their faces? Are the office doors open or closed? How's the furniture arranged, and how does that make you feel?

In other words, try to get the vibe of the place.

• Be Aware of How You Communicate on a Nonverbal Level

A good job interview, like any business meeting, is all about the exchange of information. A great deal of that information, particularly in face-to-face meetings, may be communicated through your posture, gestures and general "body language."

Nonverbal communication is a subject unto itself and beyond the scope of this book. Still, there are certain techniques beyond the opening handshake that are recommended by experts in the field and will advance your cause. Whether you're standing or in a seated position, for instance, you want to assume a balanced, even posture. Keeping your head steady with your chin parallel to the floor, moreover, similar to the way a television anchor appears when giving the news, will convey an air of stability and authority.

• Smile

A form of nonverbal communication that could well be one of Mother's Rules, the smile is important enough to be discussed on its own.

The fact is that most people forget to smile during an interview. That's certainly understandable. Interviewing is a serious business. Perhaps it's not as dire a situation as walking a tightrope between two thirty-story buildings, but it's serious nonetheless.

Still, a smile, if it's genuine, is a way of establishing a nice personal connection between you and your interviewer. Even if that person doesn't actually notice the smile, it will register with him unconsciously and help lower his defenses.

Needless to say, your smile should be natural and appropriate to the situation. Flashing a Cheshire Cat grin on and off like a neon sign is not likely to make a good impression. As your mother would tell you (assuming you're not Hitler), just be yourself!

• Be Positive

A smile, to be sure, packs a punch, but it's really just one aspect of being a positive person—a characteristic that is directly related to Fit.

Think about the people with whom you choose to socialize in life—be they significant others, friends, or close work colleagues. Chances are they share certain qualities. They're probably cheerful, energetic, engaged, and interesting, among many other things. In other words, they generate positive energy, and we all like to have people with positive energy around us.

The same principle applies to the qualities you project during a job interview. If you're a positive person, your interviewer will be more comfortable with you and be more inclined to consider the other attributes you bring to the table.

 ## COMMENT:

This is another place to talk about the importance of preparation. The more you prepare for your interview, the more secure and confident you'll be when it takes place. Such confidence will help you to be less self-conscious, be more attuned to your interviewer and the surroundings, and have a more engaged, positive approach to your interview.

• Ask Your Interviewer about Himself

At some point during your interview, perhaps during the last third of it, ask your interviewer about himself. Perhaps you'll want to ask him how long he's been with the firm and where he worked before he joined it.

More importantly, you want to ask him what he likes most about the firm or his job and what, if anything, he'd do to make the company or his job even better than it is. (Note that I've framed that second question in positive terms, as opposed to "What do you think needs to be improved about the firm?")

There are two reasons to ask these kinds of questions. The first and most obvious one is that people love to talk about themselves. Get them to expound on their favorite subject, and they'll be happy campers.

The second and more essential reason for asking these types of questions, however, is that most people, despite what you may think, *do not ask them during interviews*. As a consequence, most interviewers will not be as prepared to answer them as the standard questions they know you'll ask (and should ask) about the company and job responsibilities.

Given that lack of preparation, they'll be less likely to give you the canned, rah-rah type of answer they're used to providing. Chances are, instead, they'll be more spontaneous and provide more truthful, useful information about the workplace in the job.

CHAPTER VIII
THE CONCLUSION OF THE INTERVIEW

- ## Avoid Closing Questions

Everyone can tell when an interview is winding down. Maybe the interviewer says as much or stands up. Maybe a hook comes out, like in the old Vaudeville days. Whatever the clue, it's time to bring things to a nice, neat conclusion.

Some recruiters will advise you to ask what I call "closing questions." Those are questions such as, "What's the next step?" "How many other people have you interviewed for the position, and how do I compare to them?" "When will I hear from you?" and "Have I demonstrated my qualifications for the job?"

Those types of questions may well be appropriate for certain types of interviews. For sales positions, for example, they're almost expected.

I don't, however, recommend closing questions at the end of interview for the type of professional jobs that are the subject of this book. Not only will they not add anything truly valuable to your knowledge, they may also create a backlash.

An important rule for trial attorneys conducting cross-examination is to never ask a witness a question unless you know what the answer will be. A similar **Rule of Thumb** applies to questions during job interviews, and especially closing questions.

RULE OF THUMB:

Never ask an interviewer a question that she will not be able to answer, will feel awkward answering, or will not want to answer.

Let's say you ask how many other applicants are under consideration. Your interviewer either may not know the answer or feel that it's none of your business. Either way, you'll be putting her in an uncomfortable position and creating some friction that could have easily been avoided.

The same applies to questions about how long it will take until they follow up with you. Chances are she won't know or will not want to make promises she can't keep.

Questions about whether you've demonstrated your suitability for the job, or asking about how you compare to other applicants, are even worse. You'll be putting your interviewer on the spot for no reason and making yourself look needy in the process.

• Take Your Leave

RULE OF THUMB:

As soon as you know the interview is over, get up and get out as quickly and smoothly as you can.

One of the important social graces that all of us learn, with the exception of some out-of-state relatives, is to know when you've overstayed your welcome. That rule of etiquette applies doubly to an interview situation.

When it's clear that an interview is over, get up, thank your interviewer in a simple and professional manner, and then get the heck out of Dodge as quickly and as decisively as you can. What you actually say and do, of course, will depend on your own particular style, but something like this should suffice:

> *Thanks very much for taking the time to meet with me. I've been impressed with what I've seen and heard and look forward to hearing from you.*

With that, be sure to gather up your notebook or purse; walk purposefully toward the exit or elevator (making sure you get your parking stub validated by the receptionist, if necessary); and take your leave.

When you return to your home or office, be sure to write down a few notes, while your memory is still fresh, of what was discussed, particularly questions or areas of discussion that intrigued you, concerned you, or did not go exactly as planned. Those notes could prove invaluable if you are asked back for a call-back interview, as well as for reviewing and further improving your interview skills.

This chapter is now over. I've thoroughly enjoyed our one-way conversation and look forward to meeting you again in the next one.

CHAPTER IX
POST-INTERVIEW FOLLOW-UP

You've completed your interview, following as much of the above advice as possible, and done a reasonably good job. *Now what do you do?*

You follow up with a quick thank-you note. Then you wait.

THE THANK-YOU NOTE

The question of whether and how to send a thank-you note is one of those subjects on which recruiters and job seekers disagree. Some don't think a thank-you note is necessary. Others say that sending a note is a must. Some suggest a brief, businesslike email or letter. Others counsel a more personal approach such as a handwritten card.

The fact is that all of these suggestions may be correct. The social conventions applicable to both our business and day-to-day lives, after all, seem to be changing on an almost daily basis. Every interview, moreover, is a unique personal experience that requires a follow-up gesture appropriate to that situation.

As you may have gleaned from what you've read so far, however, I have my own take on how to handle most interview situations, including this one.

RULE OF THUMB:

Follow up on every interview by sending a written thank-you letter which is brief and businesslike.

An interview can be many things, some of which are unprintable. Fundamentally, however, it's a business meeting, even if some of the conversations you had were casual and comfortable.

Just as one should always err on the side of wearing a suit or other appropriate attire to an interview, even if it may be viewed as a little over the top, the same approach applies in a post-interview scenario. So on the very day of the interview, sit yourself down and write a concise and straightforward thank-you letter.

The wording you use, of course, will be up to you, but make sure your letter is not fawning, obsequious, verbose, or needy in any way. After all, you bring valuable experience and personal attributes to the table. Bowing down gracefully to the monarch as you take dainty steps backward may not be the best way to handle things.

What are the minimum elements you want to include? Pen your note directly to the interviewer(s) by name; thank her for her courtesy and time, and say that you look forward to hearing from her.

Some interview pundits recommend that you make reference to a particular subject you discussed, if only to show you were paying attention. That's fine as long as you hit that point extremely briefly (preferably in a single sentence) and do so in a professional, arms-length manner.

What medium should you choose for your thank-you note? An email? A "snail-mail" letter? A handwritten card?

Emails are now an accepted and almost expected aspect of business commerce. If the firm or company with which you've met is in the twenty-first century, accordingly, either an email or regular mailed letter will be fine. If, on the other hand, you've interviewed for an attorney job in an Amish community that uses horses and buggies for transportation, you should probably go with the conventional mailed letter.

You probably won't be surprised to hear in light of the above that I'm not a big fan of handwritten cards. Some people swear by them, however, and if you're one of them, have at it. Just avoid drawing flowers, and keep the exclamation points to a minimum!

If you've interviewed with several people, do you send a thank-you note to each of them or to just one of them? Again, it depends on the situation. If you can remember the names of each of the interviewers with whom you met, an individualized note to each person is preferred. If one person clearly coordinated all the interviews, however, it's perfectly acceptable to direct your letter to her and ask her to relay your thanks to all the colleagues she'd arranged for you to meet.

MAKE SURE YOUR REFERENCES ARE IN ORDER

If an employer is genuinely interested in your credentials, you will be asked for the names of at least three references. In fact, you may have already provided that information during the application process. You obligations to the employer and your-self do not stop with simply turning over a list of names, however.

You initially want to make sure that the names you provide are of work references, as opposed to friends, character wit-nesses or your mother. Employers are particularly interested in talking to individuals to whom you have reported in prior jobs, and will be justifiably suspicious of candidates whose references consist entirely of peers or subordinates.

It's equally essential, especially in today's competitive job market, that you pay attention to *unnamed references*. Many savvy employers will not stop with references you've identified, who will presumably say positive things about you. They will ask those references for names of other individu-als for and with whom you've worked, and call those indi-viduals as well. By the time you go out for your first interview, accordingly, you should have created a matrix of all possible former colleagues and supervisors who could be uncovered in a background search. Then, when feasible and discretion is absolutely assured, reach out to those individuals so that they are ready for any calls that come in.

REVIEW YOUR INTERNET PRESENCE

The growing power of the Internet and social media sites such as Facebook and LinkedIn have been a boon to pro-moting interpersonal communication and expanding our network of acquaintances. The flip side of those resources, unfortunately, is the increased accessibility others may have to your private information. You may be fond of the photo from that late night party years ago in which your girlfriend pours you a drink of tequila from her shoe. A prospective employer, however, may not be so impressed.

Being the savvy job candidate you are, you presumably scrutinized the various comments and photos posted by and about you before you arranged your first job interview. Now is the time for you to search again for anything you missed and take corrective action.

WAITING TO HEAR FROM THE EMPLOYER AND FOLLOW-UPS

Unless you're a psychotic control freak, you know there's only so much you can do when you're dealing with other people. Once you've given things your best effort, you've just got to let things go and see what happens. In other words, you have to wait.

This doesn't mean you have to be totally passive, of course. You don't have to sit on your hands for a decade hoping to hear back from the employer. At some point, you'll want to and should follow up.

• Your First Follow-Up

Assuming you don't hear from the employer right away, how long should you wait, if at all, to follow up on the status of your consideration? This is another of those calls that you have to make based on your own circumstances.

For no empirical reason other than my own anecdotal experiences as a job seeker and recruiter, I'd recommend, absent your being advised otherwise by the interviewer, that you wait about seven to ten days before you follow up. The employer, after all, will be considering other candidates, and you want to respect the time and effort that goes into the hiring process.

 ## COMMENT:

Don't get suckered into believing an interviewer when she says the employer will get back with you "soon" or within a specified period of time. Such promises, however well-intentioned when they're made, are almost never kept. In fact, if you're told that you'll hear back from the employer in, say, seven days, automatically double that time. Why is there such a disconnect between the interviewer's words and deeds when it comes to the time period for getting back to you? I haven't the foggiest idea. It's just, as the legendary newscaster Walter Cronkite used to say, "the way it is." So don't get paranoid, insulted, or even drunk if this kind of delay happens. Recognize that you have limited control over the situation. Go out for some frozen yogurt.

 ## ANOTHER COMMENT:

If you're being represented by a recruiter, it will be up to her to follow up with the employer. Although a good recruiter will do her best to keep you on the employer's radar screen, don't just assume that's happening. It's your career, your future. Stay in close touch with the recruiter, and make sure she's doing what's required to maximize your chances.

Does it make a difference whether you follow up by email or telephone? There's currently no established business protocol as to when it's appropriate to use email, as opposed to the telephone, to contact someone. Since there are no defined rules for this situation, the method you use will depend on the nature of your earlier interaction with the employer.

If you initially spoke with a partner or HR representative by phone, for example, or an interviewer encourages you to call him directly if you have any questions, then it's perfectly fine to call that individual to follow up. If you initially set up your interview by email, however, then email is the way to go at this early stage.

If the employer expresses a preference for further contacts, such as "no phone calls!" then be sure you follow that admonition. Even absent an employer's prohibition, however, I would not recommend singing telegrams. They're expensive and may not set the right tone.

• **Your Second Follow-Up**

You followed up with the employer in a timely, professional fashion ten days ago, but you haven't heard back. What do you do?

First, don't speculate about what the delay means. Employers often—and should—take their time during the hiring process. It's very possible that they're still deliberating and see no reason to contact you until they have something definitive to say.

My recommendation under such circumstances is that you give the employer the benefit of the doubt, and assume that they're approaching the decision-making process in a careful and methodical fashion. You've already demonstrated your diligence and interest in the job by sending your thank-you letter and then doing your first follow-up. Give it another week and see if they get back to you. If they don't, contact them again using the same method—email or phone call—that you used for your first follow-up, and hope that you'll get some helpful information.

• Additional Follow-Ups

Good Lord. You've followed up twice with the employer and done so in a professional manner. It's now been several weeks since your interview or since they answered earlier follow-ups by promising to get back to you. Your patience and conscientious follow-throughs have been rewarded with a big fat radio silence.

Could the continued delay mean that you're out of the running at this point? Yes, it's possible. On the other hand, even some of the best companies and firms are woefully dysfunctional when it comes to the hiring process. They may simply have not gotten their act together.

Delays by employers are particularly common, and longer in duration, during recessions. Faced with the prospect of so many qualified, eager candidates looking for a job, many employers succumb to a "browsing" compulsion, rendering them almost pathologically indecisive.

Regardless of the circumstances underlying the employer's delay in following up with you, one thing is clear. Speculation will get you nowhere.

So what do you do? Take constructive action. Pick up the phone and call the individual who coordinated your interview. If you reach that person, great. Find out whether the employer is close to concluding the hiring process and, if so, where you stand in the consideration process. These are direct and perfectly fine questions to ask, especially at this stage.

If you do not reach the intended person, leave a message with the above questions. Then send an email to that individual stating that you just wanted to follow up on your earlier voice mail (or message left with a receptionist) to find out where they are in the consideration process.

• Yet Additional Follow-Ups?

You've watched the seasons change. You've seen your children grow from toddlers to codgers. You still have yet to hear anything from the employer. What do you do?

First and foremost, don't take it personally! Given the time that's now passed, it's of course now fair to assume that you're not going to get an offer. Still, unless you suddenly jumped on someone's desk and performed a Cossack dance during your interview, the lack of a response does not mean that you are a person who is not worthy of a response. All it means, really, is that the employer didn't get back to you.

Should you speculate on why you haven't been contacted by the employer and did not even receive the courtesy of a simple "no"? No. You just need to move on and continue to explore other possibilities.

Still...most of us are only human, right? We're curious about why employers give us the silent treatment. So what's really going on?

Here's my take: There are three main reasons why candidates do not hear back from employers. The first, believe it or not, has to do with embarrassment and can be well illustrated by our dating experiences. Have you ever gone on a date with someone, only to be greeted—when you've followed up to suggest another time to get together—with one lame excuse after another ("I have a hangnail") or no response at all? Why is that?

Well, excluding my own dating history—in which a blow-off invariably demonstrated the good judgment of the woman involved—it's because people often feel a little sheepish saying "no" to someone. Concerned about hurting the feelings of the other person involved, they'll do, or avoid doing, practically anything to keep from saying that dreaded word. The net result, of course, is the opposite of what that person intended, since a simple "no" would have brought things to a cleaner and more merciful end.

Believe it or not, the same sentiment applies to some firms and companies, even large, prominent ones. The people in charge of the hiring process, rightly or wrongly, don't want to hurt an applicant's feelings by rejecting her. So, they do nothing, which of course leaves the candidate hanging and feeling frustrated.

The second reason employers don't provide candidates with a definitive answer arises from simple dysfunction. The hiring principals or their hiring personnel, especially those considering a large number of candidates for an opening, simply lack the time or organizational skills to get back to every applicant.

The third reason, of course, is simple rudeness. The employer doesn't feel you or any other rejected candidate is worth the trouble of an answer, so they do nothing.

 RED FLAG:

Hopefully, you won't find yourself in the position of never hearing back from, or being strung along by, an employer who has no intention of hiring you. Should that happen, however, count yourself as fortunate. Really. You do not want to work for an organization that lacks the spine, organizational know-how, or rudimentary courtesy to tell you they've decided to hire someone else. This is particularly the case when you interview with a large organization which has its own recruiting or HR department. A failure to provide with you with any response whatsoever under those circumstances, even a simple "no," is unprofessional and inexcusable.

 **COMMENT:**

It's worth repeating (or I wouldn't be doing it) that the absolute bottom line when you don't hear back from an employer is to not take it personally. Just move on—hopefully with the resolution that when you land that dream job in the future and find yourself sitting in the interviewer's seat, you'll treat your candidates with more professionalism. Of course, if you ascribe to the magnanimous spirit of forgiveness that I've learned from my father ("Todd, I can forgive, but I NEVER FORGET!"), then you can feel free to mention how the employer treated you, in a

factual and nonjudgmental way, to every human being you have the occasion to meet between now and the end of time.

ANOTHER FOLLOW-UP SCENARIO: THE COMPETING OFFER

Let's say that, as is often the case, you're interviewing with several employers at the same time. While you're waiting to hear back from Employer B, with whom you interviewed two weeks ago and in whom you're very interested, a reasonable offer comes in from Employer A, another firm you interviewed with earlier in the process.

You really like Employer B but don't want to lose the offer from Employer A. What do you do?

Immediately inform Employer B about the pending offer, without disclosing any of the specific details. Tell Employer B that while the offer from Employer A is attractive, you remain very interested in B and don't want to pull out of the consideration process prematurely. Make it clear to B that while you don't want to put any pressure on them, you're now in a ticking clock situation, with A wanting to hear back from you within two weeks. Would it be possible for B to give you a sense, in terms of timing, where you are in the consideration process?

If Employer B is truly interested in you, they will appreciate the information you provided and, hopefully, get back to you within the time period you specified. You need to recognize, however, that you have very little control of the situation. If B doesn't get back to you as quickly as you'd prefer, all you can do, short of following up with B again (and you should), is to write them off and decide, independently, whether you want to pursue the offer from A.

CHAPTER X
THE CALL-BACK INTERVIEW

There are the privileged few out there who receive offers during their first visit to an employer. The rest of us, if we're lucky, will be called back for a further round(s) of interviews.

• Preparing for Call-Back Interviews

The implications of call-back interviews are many. The underlying strategy for preparing for such interviews, on the other hand, is eminently simple.

 **RULE OF THUMB:**

A call-back interview is really a first interview.

That's really all there is to it. Putting this concept into action, of course, will require considerable work on your part, just as it would for a first interview. This preparation means, at a minimum, that you will:

1. Review your knowledge of the position and the firm or company (chapter 2).

2. Try to recall, in as much detail as possible, everything that was said during your first interview visit.

3. Think of open-ended, substantive questions to ask during the call-back interview. These questions could well include some of the same questions you asked during your first interview, but which you'll now direct to other people in the organization. You should also have some follow-up and completely new questions to ask (chapter 4).

4. Take your resume out and read it as if for the first time. Try to anticipate questions that an interviewer may ask you about your skills and experience. Review and actually articulate how you would answer those questions in lay, easy-to-understand terms; that is, as if you were talking with someone who knows nothing about you or your profession (chapter 6).

5. Review all of the tough question-and-answer scenarios we talked about in chapter 5, and try to come up with others that we haven't discussed. Review and actually articulate how you'd answer those questions (chapter 2).

6. Remember the golden rules of thumb applicable to any answer you give, especially the substantive ones about your skills and experience. Be sure that your answer to every question is:

- **R**ESPONSIVE TO THE QUESTION ASKED

- **C**OMPLETE IN AND OF ITSELF

- **I**NTERESTING

- **U**PBEAT, and

- **C**ONCISE (chapter 6)

7. Dress appropriately and arrive in the reception area about seven to ten minutes before the interview is scheduled to begin (chapter 3).

8. Be very aware of the importance of Fit to both the company's consideration of you and your consideration of it (chapter 7).

9. As soon as it's clear that the interview has ended, leave the employer's premises as quickly, smoothly, and professionally as you can (chapter 8).

10. Send your thank-you letter and follow up as appropriate (chapter 9).

• Additional Considerations for Call-Back Interviews

If you've made it to this part of the book, you're undoubtedly one of those pesky conscientious types who always has more questions, even when guiding principles have been laid out as lucidly and beautifully as they are above. So let's take some of your likely concerns:

1. *Do I really have to do all of the same preparation I did for the first interview?*

   Complete preparation is the Platonic Ideal, but every person's circumstances are different. The point here is for you to do as much preparation as possible. If your first and call-back interviews are only one week apart, for example, some of your earlier preparation may still be fresh in your mind. Preparation is still important, but may take a little less time—perhaps forty-five minutes as opposed to the hour you spent getting ready for the first interview.

The best example I can give here goes back to my days as a trial attorney. There were plenty of occasions during which I had prepared hard for a trial or complicated hearing, only to have the court postpone the proceeding for a week or more due to other pressing matters.

Regardless of whether the delay lasted one week or one month, and even though I had a pretty good memory back then, I always made the point to do nearly the same type and amount of preparation before the next scheduled court appearance. This meant, at least given my obsessive-compulsive preparation style, that I'd individually review, and sometimes even rework, all the questions I had planned to ask each witness and the arguments I'd give to the court or jury if certain situations came up. Even if I knew the case inside and out, this type of preparation, as tedious as it sometimes was, would make all the facts once again fresh in my mind. It also ensured that once I was back in court, I would be able to make my points in a clear, concise, and persuasive manner.

Perhaps you have a better memory than I and don't have to adopt the same plodding, methodical approach. That's fine. The key here is to realize that you probably won't be as prepared as you think you are.

A follow-up job interview, just like a first interview, is one of the most important, and potentially life-changing, business meetings you'll ever have. It deserves every bit as much preparation as you put in for a crucial, difficult exam during college.

2. *Should I be concerned about asking or saying the same things I did last time? I don't want to bore the interviewers or have them think I can't come up with something new.*

Don't be concerned. Most employers are not as good at interviewing as you would expect them to be (see chapter 5). Consequently, don't assume that the first interviewer has completely briefed the second interviewer(s) on what transpired during your initial meeting. Don't even assume that she relayed any information at all or that your subsequent interviewers even looked at your resume more than two minutes before you walked into the room. So, if the questions and answers you provided during your first interview were effective and relevant to the next interview, do not hesitate to use them.

A good example of what I'm talking about comes from the public relations world. Let's say a bank president is facing a scandal resulting from some dishonest bank tellers stealing personal information, and then money, from the bank's customers. When the bank's PR person prepares the president to go before the media, she'll carve out two or three main "talking points" for him to emphasize, such as the facts that the tellers were rogue criminals acting on their own, did not have criminal records that would have alerted the bank to future problems when they were hired, and that the bank itself came forward and brought the facts to the police as soon as the crime came to its attention.

When the bank president subsequently fields questions from reporters, you'll see him emphasize those talking points again and again, almost regardless of what he's asked. You've probably noticed politicians doing the same thing when they run for office. Consider using this same technique when you get in trouble with your spouse. (Of course my wife, who will be reading this, knows I'm totally kidding about that last point.)

3. *But what if I'm meeting with one of the same interviewers I talked with last time, or he's in the room? Should I stay away from things I said earlier?*

Remember the example of the bank president and his talking points. You bring certain experience, skills, and other assets to the table. They're your strengths, your talking points. If you don't emphasize them, perhaps with a rephrasing here and there, you're doing yourself a disservice.

Also, don't assume that your earlier interviewer remembers every word of his meeting with you. It's very possible that the earlier interviewer did not take extensive notes of his conversation with you or has since talked to several other candidates, blurring his recollection of any particular discussion.

If you've done your preparation, moreover, you're going to be fresh, ready, and spontaneous in your next interviews. You won't have to worry about sounding like you're mindlessly reciting exactly what you said last time. You will no doubt have also come up with a few new gems of questions or information to lay on your interviewers.

CHAPTER XI
ODDS AND ENDS

This book is intended to prepare you for your interview as quickly and comprehensively as possible without making your head explode. With that in mind, I'm going to randomly address a few other issues that can come up in interviews, and then open up the floor for questions.

• Humor

Humor is one of those great things in life that ties us together while also showcasing our individuality. Since each person's sense of humor is different (sometimes to the point of being peculiar, as amply illustrated by this book), you never know how someone is going to react. So it's best to stay away from it during a job interview.

This recommendation doesn't mean you have to be dour, however. It's perfectly fine to gently point out something amusing during a conversation if it's appropriate and doesn't paint anyone or anything in a negative light.

The lesson? Just use your best judgment and avoid going for the guffaws.

• Politics and Religion

The reasons for avoiding these subjects are self-evident. You never know exactly what an individual's beliefs are, and if they aren't the same, you run the risk of offending him.

Even if the interviewer has a photo and fifteen banners featuring your favorite presidential candidate on the wall, don't go there. The interviewer may well agree with you, but nevertheless feel you're being unprofessional by bringing up a subject that most candidates know to avoid.

• Chumminess

All firms and companies have their own personalities. Interviewers reflect this diversity, with communication styles ranging from formal and party line to casual and irreverent.

Interviewers on the more formal side of the spectrum tend, by their very nature, to conduct more conventional, predictable interviews. That's actually fine as far as you're concerned, because you'll at least have a better idea of where the conversation is going and how to provide the information requested.

The danger lies with the interviewers on the more casual side of the scale. Whether warm and friendly by nature or scheme, they'll appeal to your instinctive wish to be liked and part of the cadre.

It's perfectly fine to adapt your conversational style to your interviewer's personality but only within reason. Do not fall to the temptation of getting too informal or casual with him. All people, however informal they may appear, have boundaries. Unless you've known your interviewer for years or are a mind reader, you'll have no idea where he draws those lines.

The lesson? It's simple. Be warm, receptive, and friendly, but do not be chummy!

• **Selling Yourself**

"I think I'm right for this job because I'm a real people person. Now, are you going to hire me or not? I don't have all freakin' day!"

Some how-to books suggest that candidates emphasize positive personal qualities at some point during an interview, such as, "I'm a very hard worker," "I'm very energetic and loyal to my company and colleagues," and "I'm excellent at building relationships."

I disagree. There's only a marginal chance that making such statements during an interview (or in a resume, for that matter) will help you, and there's a greater probability that they'll be counterproductive.

An illustration of why this is the case comes from, as do many things, my dating history. I once went out with a woman who shared some advice that her mother had given her: If a man ever told her to "trust me" during the course of the relationship, she should break up with him immediately. I politely disagreed, stating that each person should be treated on his own merits, and that I was a trustworthy person.

After this woman dumped me, I had the time to consider the wisdom of her mother's advice. It should go without saying that a person works hard, gets along well with people, and is loyal and trustworthy. If he has to go to the point of explicitly pointing that out in a conversation, it's a sign that he's trying too hard and that something about him may just be a little off.

There are exceptions to every rule, of course. Nevertheless, the customary objective of every job interview is to relate the experience, skills, and smarts that qualify you for the job. You shouldn't have to volunteer that you're an honest person and have never done time in prison, because you may be creating a red flag for a personal failing that does not exist.

Trust me on this. I'm a very diligent and honest recruiter and have never given anyone anything less than perfect advice.

• Assessing Your Performance at an Interview

It's always a good idea to evaluate how you handled an interview after the fact. I go through that process with my candidates all the time.

Still, it's one thing to examine the specifics of what happened at an interview for the purpose of honing your skills. It's quite another to predict how the interview was perceived by the other party. This leads us to a

RULE OF THUMB:

You can never predict how well you did at an interview. You may believe you rocked their world, only to find out that you've been excluded from consideration, or believe you performed poorly, only to learn that the employer can't wait to contact you with an offer.

What's the lesson here? It's to recognize the limits of your ability to control outside events. You did the best you could under the circumstances, and it is the right of the employer—whether rightly or wrongly, wisely or foolishly—to decide if it wants to bring you aboard. All you can do is continue the other aspects of your job search while you wait to hear back from the employer.

• The Interview Teaser

Not everyone who conducts an interview, as you've probably noticed from your own experience, is the sharpest tool in the shed. One notable and lame subspecies of this group is an individual I'll call the "Interview Teaser."

The Interview Teaser will express immense enthusiasm about your candidacy. Whether motivated by the excitement of the moment or ineptitude, he will nearly convince you that you've landed the job, even when that's far from the truth.

One telltale sign of an Interview Teaser is his working hard to sell you on the firm or company. Another is his giving you a warm, all-embracing tour of the office, including introductions to many of his work colleagues.

Yet another occurs when, usually during a first interview, he decides to bring one of the Big Cheeses at the firm into the meeting, even though that person had not been expected to participate. Still other Interview Teasers will go as far as to introduce you to "your office," "your secretary," and eagerly brief you on the firm's benefits and even parking arrangements.

Don't get sucked in. Some interviewers simply express some of the standard features of the job in an artless, excessively personal way. Others genuinely want to bring you aboard, only to later be distracted by other candidates or decision makers.

The lesson? An interview is a business meeting, not a play date. Interpret all statements and actions from an arms-length, objective perspective.

• If an Employer Decides Not to Hire You

You may understandably feel disappointed or rejected if an employer passes on your candidacy, but don't take it personally. The applicable decision makers have simply reached a conclusion, based on their own criteria, that you're not the person for the job. They may have made the wrong decision (which often happens, and why we recruiters have a livelihood!), but it's their decision nonetheless.

If your contacts at the employer do not give you the reasons for not moving forward with you—and they almost never will—there's no sense in contacting them to see if they'll give you those reasons or a critique of your performance. They won't, and you'll only frustrate yourself.

The lesson? Bottom-line it. The employer is not going to hire you, and the interview process has stopped. Accept it and move on!

• **The Thank-You-For-Rejecting-Me Letter**

What should you do when you learn you've been rejected by an employer? Well, you could do nothing and go off to nurse your wounds. That's a common and perfectly acceptable response.

The better option, however, is to send a brief, businesslike note to the main person(s) who interviewed you, telling her that you've been notified of the firm's decision and that you appreciate her time and consideration of your candidacy.

Why in the world would you do this, other than out of a sheer streak of masochism? Because an interview, no matter how it turns out, is one of the most intense networking opportunities out there. Chances are that the interviewer was impressed with you, but just ultimately concluded that someone else was better suited to the job.

It's not unknown for a former candidate to run into his interviewer at some point in the future and even become friends with her under other circumstances. It's even possible that one day, after you've landed that next job, that the tables will have turned and you'll find yourself actually interviewing *her* for a position at your employer!

The lesson here? Accept a rejection as final and move on, but do so in a gracious manner that doesn't burn any bridges.

• Other Types of Job Interviews and Business Meetings

I made a point at the beginning of this book to explain that our discussion would be limited to job interviews, as opposed to the preparation of resumes or other aspects related to a job search. Still, once you master the principles for successful job interviews, you'll find them readily applicable to other situations. Let's look at some examples:

1.   Interviewing for a Sales Position

The interview techniques in this book, while targeted to "professionals" such as attorneys, accountants, HR advisors and doctors, are applicable to most types of jobs. There are certain types of occupations, however, which require a slightly different tactical approach to ensure interview success. The most prominent of these are sales positions.

As you'll recall from Chapter VII (and if not, you'd better review it now — it *just may* be on the exam), I recommend that candidates interviewing for professional jobs avoid "closing questions" intended to pressure the interviewer into hiring them on the spot. The fact is that the people who conduct the interviews for professional jobs tend to be— whether rightly or wrongly—chronically unwilling or unable to make a commitment during a job interview. Under such circumstances, an innocuous question about other people the employer may be considering, or even an attempt to secure a callback interview, may be viewed as unduly needy or pushy, and jeopardize the candidate's chances.

Such delicate rules of etiquette do not apply to interviews for sales positions. Sales candidates are *expected* to go for a "hard close" at the conclusion of the interview which, at a minimum, requires a strong expression of interest in the job and eagerness to start immediately. They will often ask the interviewer whether they've demonstrated they have all the qualifications required for the job, and if not, what issues haven't been covered that they should immediately address. It's not unusual, in fact, for a good sales candidate to ask for the job at the conclusion of the interview, and, upon receiving anything short of an unconditional "yes," press the interviewer on the immediate steps to take to ensure that this obviously correct and preordained result occurs.

So if you have an interview coming up for a sales position, you should find the tactics in this book to be useful and effective. Plan, however, for a harder close at the meeting's end. It will be expected by the interviewer, and may just land you the job.

2.   Business Meeting to Pitch a New Client or Investor

A job interview, reduced to its basic elements, is simply a form of business meeting, the subject of which is your entering into an employment relationship with a firm or company. So it should come as no surprise that when you compare the techniques in this book to the advice that corporate coaches give to executives before important business development meetings, the recommendations are nearly the same.

Whether you're a job candidate or a business professional preparing for an important meeting, for example, you need to do your Internal Preparation and have a genuine understanding of your core business objectives. You also need to do your External Research to learn as much as you can about the company or individual with whom you'll be meeting. Just as a job candidate should review her resume and practice articulating how her qualifications match the job, moreover, you should know your background, experience and qualifications cold, and then practice articulating how you will employ them to further your new client's or investor's interests.

You must also walk into the room with open-ended, substantive questions to help you learn more about the person(s) on the other side of the table. You must prepare not only for both expected areas of discussion, but for tricky questions about weaknesses, prior failures, comparisons with your competitors, and any other questions, whether savvy or clueless, which may be thrown at you by the party on the other side of the table.

There is one aspect of a business meeting that differs from most of the interview scenarios in this book, however, and should be handled differently. A meeting arranged to attract new business or clients is more similar to an interview for a sales job than it is to an interview for a professional position such as an attorney or accountant. Your best bet under such circumstances is to go for a harder close at the meeting's conclusion. Either ask for the business, or inquire about the next concrete steps required for that objective to be achieved.

3.   Interviews for Colleges and Universities

The similarity between an interview for a position at a company and admission to an institution of higher learning is self-evident. The key issue in both types of meetings will be your qualifications and compatibility for the school involved, and your success will turn on the quality of your internal preparation and research of the institution and its requirements. Like any good job interview candidate, you'll need to prepare intelligent, open-ended questions to ask at the meeting, and anticipate both the standard and tricky questions that may be thrown your way. You'll also need to observe professional etiquette in concluding your meeting, send a thank you note, and then follow-up periodically until you've hopefully obtained the desired result.

4.   Visa Interviews

Let's say you're an Indian citizen applying for a tourist visa to visit the United States, or an American student applying for a visa to study abroad in Russia. The same principles apply. You need to be clear about the type of visa you're seeking, and research the requirements and procedures followed in the consulate of the country you'd like to visit. Then prepare your answers to anticipated areas of inquiry and have questions of your own ready on key points.

Let's look at a resident of Mumbai who's planning his first trip to the United States to tour its major cities and national parks. Whether rightly or wrongly, many U.S. consular officials believe citizens of other countries want nothing less than to become U.S. residents, using tourist visas as a ruse to enter the country, blend into the diverse American population, and apply for a U.S. Permanent Resident card ("green card") at some later time.

The would-be tourist from Mumbai has to prepare for that American mindset, however justified or unjustified it may be. That means that he'll be ready for questions about how long he'll be in the United States, the cities he plans to visit, and the hotels or friends or relatives he knows or plans to visit there. He must also be ready to answer questions about his family, occupation and other ties to Mumbai, and all the wonderful things that will prompt a timely return home at the planned end of his trip.

Similar challenges face a New York-born dancer who wants to study at the world-famous Vaganova Academy of Russian Ballet in St. Petersburg, Russia. She will be closely questioned on her planned course of study, contacts and connections to Russia and to the United States, and long-term plans. Given the differences between the two countries' political systems, moreover, she may need to prepare for political questions regarding her beliefs and agenda, as well as her familiarity with the obligations of foreign citizens who have been granted student visas there.

The individual questions and requirements applicable to a visa interview can of course be as distinctive as the different countries themselves. The level of preparation and good technique required for success, however, is identical to that for a job interview.

5.   Media Appearances

Having taken the time to read this book, you are clearly an individual of superior intelligence and judgment. You've no doubt detected a running theme here, then: Follow the rules for effective job interviews, and you'll be well prepared for many other types of business endeavors. Let's look at another example: the media interview.

With the increasing prevalence of cable, satellite and Internet-transmitted print, audio and video communications comes the fact that more of us are obtaining public exposure than in days past. Perhaps you or your company are being profiled in a local mini-blog. Perhaps you've written an article on a topic to promote your business or professional profile. Perhaps you need to appear at a press conference, either to promote a positive new development or to respond to unfortunate publicity.

Whatever the situation, you will need to communicate your position in a clear and positive manner. That means you must analyze and understand the short and long-term goals you want to accomplish; research the media outlets and individuals with which you will be communicating; and identify and rehearse the key positive facts or attributes (called "talking points" in the media biz) that you will need to highlight. You must also be prepared for all types of questions—logical tricky and ridiculous; dress conservatively and appropriately; and make sure your nonverbal cues match your verbal message.

Needless to say, the above is an oversimplification. There are unique aspects to media events that are beyond the scope of this book. There are many consultants in the public relations and media training area who are excellent and may be worth contacting in the appropriate circumstances.

6. Pitching a Book, Screenplay or Other Project

In even broaching this subject, I am perhaps committing one of the mistakes I've cautioned you to avoid during job interviews—exaggerating your experience or attempting to answer questions that you are not qualified to answer. My expertise, after all, is in the area of executive recruiting and interview coaching. Until such time as I decide to enter a field in which hard-earned experience or knowledge of one's limitations is irrelevant—politics, for example—prudence dictates that I hew to the topic of job interviewing.

With the above cautions in mind, however, the techniques in this book will be helpful in fashioning a pitch for your project. A pitch meeting, after all, is yet another variety of business meeting. Clear, concise and engaging communications skills are essential. As with job interviews, one needs to have one's goals clearly defined (Internal Preparation), a familiarity with the company, people and individuals with which you will be meeting based on solid research (External Preparation), and a ready capability to discuss your concept honed by practice. You'll need to be prepared to discuss your experience and credits, and answer questions about the potential markets and commercial viability of your project.

The Five Rules of Thumb for Answering Substantive Questions apply as well. As in a job interview, you need to listen to and provide a response that is not only directly relevant to the question asked, but is also interesting, upbeat, complete and concise.

It is in the actual content of the pitch, however, where the rules of this book and an entertainment-related pitch project diverge. Many experts in the entertainment field emphasize the need to tell an engaging, visual story starting with an emotional hook and ending with a compelling conclusion.

As is the case for media interviews and the other scenarios discussed above, the methods offered in this *Guide* provide a solid framework for preparing and effectively presenting your case in a variety of contexts. You'll then need to add additional elements unique to each of those other fields, with the guidance, when appropriate, of books or coaches with expertise in those areas.

7.   Relationships

There are some obvious similarities between how one goes about preparing for a job interview and creating personal relationships. Whether going out on a first date or meeting one's in-laws for example, it's helpful to have accurate self-knowledge and be comfortable in one's own skin, pay attention to dress and etiquette, and to have researched the person you'll be meeting. Other than these clear distinctions, however (and knowing that my wife will be reading this book), I know when I'm beyond my pay grade... Consult the experts!

CHAPTER XII
CONCLUDING THOUGHTS

L et's end our little conversation, as we began it, with a few
provisos.

• Interviewing Is an Art, Not a Science

The purpose of this book is to give you as many helpful hints as
possible for engaging in a job interview. Interviewing is an art,
however, not a science, and no two interviews are identical.

Many recruiters and interview pundits may suggest differing
approaches to handling problems, and in some cases, all
of those approaches may be right. It's you who will be on
the spot during an interview and will have to meet the challenges as best you can.

With that said, there is one universal truth on which all interview experts agree.

 **UNIVERSAL RULE OF THUMB:**

*Do your preparation. Interviewing is like driving a
race car. You may have incredible natural instincts*

and talent, but if you don't train and prepare for contingencies, you'll be in one heap of trouble.

So what's the lesson here? Do your preparation!

• Negotiating Offers

Negotiating an offer is obviously a hugely significant issue but beyond the scope of this book. This book is intended as a guide to conducting the most effective interview possible. It is not an encyclopedia of the entire job-search process. My mission is to get you to that offer and give you the tools for evaluating whether the offer and, more importantly, the employer, is worth your consideration.

There are of course many books and lectures available on how to negotiate compensation packages and many other things. Feel free to consult them. Alternatively, you can wait for my book on the subject, which I can confidently commit to bringing out sometime between next year and the end of time.

• Life After Accepting the Offer

Job interviews, offers, and acceptances, for all their importance, are only the preliminaries for your moving into another position and taking the next crucial step in your professional and personal life.

First impressions and first decisions at the workplace will play a key role in your ultimate job success, whether rightly or wrongly. There are plenty of resources that provide advice on this next phase of your career, and you should consider consulting them.

• Thanks

Thanks for listening. You've been an attentive, if somewhat quiet, audience!

ABOUT THE AUTHOR

Todd Moster is a 1982 graduate of UCLA School of Law. He served as a Deputy District Attorney for the Kern County District Attorney's Office for four years. Upon entering private practice in 1987, he represented clients in business, real estate and employment litigation matters and became a partner at Donfeld, Kelley & Rollman, a well-regarded Los Angeles law firm. He has tried numerous cases to verdict, and presided over small claims and traffic cases as a Judge Pro Tem.

Todd left the practice of law in 1998 to become an executive recruiter specializing in the legal industry. He worked for two of the largest recruiting companies in the world, Robert Half International and Hudson Legal, before founding his own legal search firm, Moster Legal Placement, Inc. (http://mosterlegal.com), in 2008. His company recruits and finds jobs for high-level legal professionals on a permanent and contract basis.

As a recruiter, Todd has prepared hundreds of people for job interviews. He's placed a variety of legal professionals into jobs with law firms and corporations, including law firm partners and associates, in-house corporate attorneys, paralegals, HR administrators and marketing directors. His company additionally offers a specialized coaching service, Interview BootCamp® (http://www.mosterlegal.com/Bootcamp.html), which provides training to people in all types of careers in effective job interviewing techniques.

Todd has also worked in documentary television, including as a writer for the popular History Channel show, The Great Ships. He lives in Los Angeles, California with his wife Roxanne.

ACKNOWLEDGMENTS

So many generous people have provided their time, feedback and support to me in writing the First and Second Editions of *The Underground Guide* that naming them all would be an exercise of futility for me and tedium for the reader. Among those who deserve special mention, however, are Bill Saleebey, Ph.D., an expert on business networking and author of *Connecting: Beyond the Name Tag*, for reading this book in its first draft and providing constructive feedback on both the book's content and the publishing process; Mark Goulston, M.D., the author of (among many other books) *Just Listen: Discover the Secret to Getting Through to Absolutely Anyone* and *Get Out of Your Own Way* (with coauthor Phillip Goldberg), for his personal insights and encouragement; Executive Coaches and Business Advisors David Ackert and Gideon Grunfeld, Esq., who provided valuable advice on the content and marketing strategy for the book; Drs. Janet and Neal Larsen Palmer, the Founders of the Communication Excellence Institute, for their expertise on the importance of nonverbal communication in the business settings, which served as the basis of the new material on that subject included in Chapter VII, and for their gracious support for my endeavors; Steve Goldstein, longtime friend and President of Payroll Management Solutions, for his consistent encouragement and expertise on interviews for sales positions; and Chris Malburg, best-selling business writer, financial wiz, novelist and author of *Surviving the Bond Bear Market* (with coauthor Marilyn Cohen) and *How to Fire Your Boss*, for his guidance on the book and basic generosity of time and spirit. I must also give special mention to Godfrey (Jeff) Harris, President of the Harris/Ragan Management Group. A prolific author, former U.S. Army Intelligence Officer, U.S. Foreign Service Officer and official in the Lyndon Johnson Administration, Jeff is also a highly regarded book publisher who, among other things, crafts domestic and international book distribution deals. Jeff has served as an editor and mentor in preparing this second and more globally-oriented edition. His feedback, many helpful suggestions and support have been invaluable and much appreciated.

I'm especially grateful to my wife Roxanne, without whose love, support, and excellent editing skills this book would not have been written.

Finally, I'd like to gratefully acknowledge all of the mistakes, blunders, and gaffes I've had the opportunity to personally encounter during my professional life as an attorney and occasional job seeker. While truly too numerous (and embarrassing) to name, they've provided the lessons and groundwork on which a rewarding career as an executive recruiter—and a useful primer on the job interview process—has been based.

Appendix:
INTERVIEW PREPARATION AND PRACTICE GUIDE

A.

LIST OF SAMPLE INTERVIEW QUESTIONS

The following is a list of questions that often come up in job interview situations. Keep in mind that this list is not exhaustive since the content and phrasing of questions asked in interviews can be as varied as the job opportunities and personalities of the people involved. Still, the following should provide a good starting-point for familiarizing yourself with the interview process, and help you anticipate the types of questions you must be prepared to address.

1. General Questions about Current Job, Work Experience and Educational Background

- Tell me about your current position. What are your responsibilities?

- To whom do you report? Does anybody report to you?

- [If you supervise people:] Describe how you supervise people. What types of tasks do you delegate to others and how do you do it?

- Describe a typical day in your job.

- What major accomplishments have you had in your present position/career?

- What specific experience do you have that qualifies you for this position?

- What specific skills do you have that qualify you for this position?

- What is your educational background?

- [If asked about college grades and they were not spectacular:] Tell me about your grades and why they weren't higher.

- Have you had any other training or background that is relevant to this position?

- [If you've worked at several different jobs in the past:] It looks like you have a lot of movement on your resume. Can you explain why you've changed jobs so many times?

- [If there are gaps in your work history:] I notice that there is a time on your resume in which you apparently were not working. What were you doing during that time?

- Do you have references available that we can call? Who are they?

- If we were to call your supervisor and ask about you, what would he say?

2.   Personal Questions About You

- Tell me about yourself.

- Describe your organizational style.

- How do you go about making important decisions?

- Why are you looking for a job?

- Why are you looking to leave your current job?

- What do you do in your free time? Do you have any hobbies?

- What long-range objectives do you have for your life and career?

- What would your ideal job be?

- Where do you see yourself in five years? Ten years?

- What kind of magazines do you read?

- What's the last book you read?

- What famous person would you most like to meet?

3. Questions about your Interview Preparation and Career Objectives

- Why did you apply for this position?

- How did you hear about us?

- What do you know about us?

- How does the position you're interviewing for compare to what you're doing in your present job?

- What do you seek to accomplish in this position?

- What are your long-term goals for working here?

4. Tough and Tricky Questions

- How much money are you looking to make?

- What are you currently being paid?

- Why do you want to leave your current job?

- Was there any one event at work that prompted you to start exploring other opportunities?

- [If applicable:] Why have you changed jobs so often?

- How many other employers are you talking with?

- Who else have you interviewed with?

- How long have you been looking?

- Why do you want to work here?

- Have you ever been terminated from a job? If so, what were the circumstances?

- What are your top three strengths?

- What are your top three weaknesses?

- What do you least like about your present job/ profession?

- What's the greatest challenge or difficulty you face in your current job?

- What would you improve about your current job/ profession if you could?

- What's the worst thing that has ever happened to you in your job/profession?

- What are the biggest risks you've taken in the course of your career, and how did things work out?

- What's the biggest mistake you've ever made in your job/profession, and how did you deal with it?

- What's the most uncomfortable or awkward situation you've had to deal with in your job/profession?

- What really bothers you about your job/profession?

- What's the worst dispute you've had with someone in the workplace and how did you deal with it?

- Have you ever had a disagreement on an ethical issue with a supervisor or coworker, and if so, how did you deal with it?

- How do you take criticism? Can you give me an example of some recent significant criticism you've received, and how you responded to it?

- What types of people do you find most difficult to work with?

- How do you handle last-minute assignments or challenges? Can you give me an example?

- What famous person would you most like to meet? Why?

- What quality or aspect of your personality would people who don't know you well find most surprising?

5. Oddball Questions (often asked to gauge creativity, problem-solving skills or ability to respond to unexpected or frustrating situations)

- if you were going to compare yourself to a certain breed of dog or cat, what type would it be and why?

- If you could live in a different time or place in world history, when and where would it be and why?

- Who was your favorite comic book or cartoon character when you were growing up?

- If you had to spend the rest of your life on a desert island with one famous person, who would that person be?

- If all the electrical power in the country were to stop running suddenly for the next 30 days, what is the very first thing you would do? What's the second thing you would do?

- What is your favorite cuisine, and what does that say about your personality?

B.

RATINGS CRITERIA FOR EVALUATING PRACTICE ANSWERS

Anticipating the types of questions that you will be asked in a job interview is a crucial part of your preparation process, but only the first step. You must then refine your planned answers and hone your delivery style through practice. For most people, that means articulating your answers out loud.

There are many different ways in which job candidates rehearse their interview responses, and you should choose the method most comfortable for you. Some talk to themselves in an empty room and/or into a mirror. Others record their answers in audio or video format. Still others have a family member, friend or acquaintance ask them the questions and listen to their responses.

Whatever practice method you choose, it is equally important that you, or the person helping you, then evaluate the quality of your answers. Suggested ratings criteria are provided below for that purpose. Use these factors to evaluate the content, delivery and presentation aspects of your interview style on a scale of 1-10, with 1 being the weakest and least effective response, and 10 being the strongest and most effective response.

1.   Answer Content, Format and Delivery

- Length/Conciseness of Answer

- Responsiveness of Answer to Question Asked or Subject Being Discussed

- Familiarity with Material

- Use/Non-Use of Technical Jargon

- Clarity

- Interesting/Engaging Nature of Content

- Communication of Upbeat/Positive Attitude

- Self-contained Nature (i.e., beginning, middle and end) of Answer

- Spontaneity

- Persuasiveness

- Warmth

- Enthusiasm

- Cadence, Volume, Smoothness of Content Delivery

2. **Nonverbal Communication**

- Handshake

- Eye Contact

- Posture

- Open gestures and body language

- Smile

Index

www.ingramcontent.com/pod-product-compliance
Lightning Source LLC
Chambersburg PA
CBHW051501170526
45166CB00001B/329